Scottish Heinemann Maths

Textbook

Heinemann Educational Publishers
Halley Court, Jordan Hill, Oxford OX2 8EJ
a division of Harcourt Education Ltd

Heinemann is a registered trademark of Harcourt Education Ltd

Writing team
John T Blair
Percy W Farren
Myra A Pearson
John W Thayers
David K Thomson

First Published 2003

08 07
10 9 8 7 6

ISBN 978 0 435179 87 8

Designed and typeset by Aqua Design Partners.
Illustrated by David Till, David Kearney, Derek Brazell,
Diane Fawcett, Tony O'Donnell, Jon Mitchell, Andy Peters and
Aqua Design Partners.
Cover Illustation by James Elston.
Printed and bound in China through Phoenix Offset

Contents

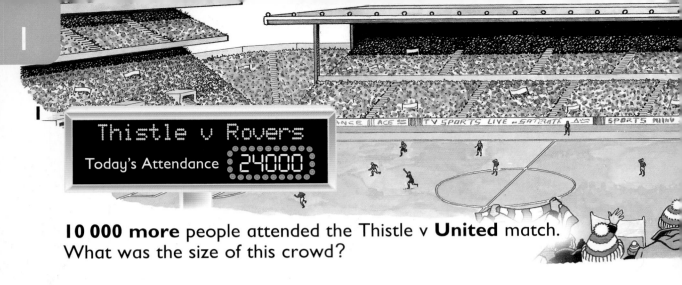

Thistle v Rovers
Today's Attendance 24000

1 **10 000 more** people attended the Thistle v **United** match.
What was the size of this crowd?

2 Write the number 10 000 more than
(a) 60 000 (b) 37 489 (c) 90 000 (d) 141 000

3 Write the number 10 000 less than
(a) 70 000 (b) 58 673 (c) 15 000 (d) 200 000

4

Weekly Sport

Thistle v Rovers—
Ticket Sales total £120 000

Ticket sales for the Thistle v **United** match
totalled **£100 000 more**.
How much did this crowd pay for tickets?

5 Write the amount £100 000 more than
(a) £700 000 (b) £350 000 (c) £900 000 (d) £404 000

6 Write the amount £100 000 less than
(a) £600 000 (b) £870 000 (c) 1 000 000 (d) £111 111

7 SporTV paid £3 000 000 to film matches last season and
£1 000 000 more this season.
How much did SporTV pay to film matches this season?

8 Find £1 000 000 more than
(a) £5 000 000 (b) £17 000 000
(c) £8 500 000 (d) £9 006 006

9 Find £1 000 000 less than
(a) £4 000 000 (b) £16 000 000
(c) £10 200 000 (d) £4 400 044

1 What is the value of the 3 in each person's score?

FROGGER	Scores
Peter	94 361
Gill	135 028
Raqia	645 932

BREAKOUT	Scores
Samia	5 318 640
Dev	3 900 275
Joan	7 046 923

2 What is the value of the **red** digit in each number?

FROGGER

(a) 192 643

(b) 607 534

(c) 1 624 758

(d) 4 600 318

(e) 6 701 542

(f) 4 535 247

(g) 8 637 190

(h) 10 563 525

(i) 13 178 624

3 BREAKOUT

2 980 374	3 890 684	2 210 748

3 980 172	3 210 650	1 809 536	1 980 374

2 809 763	4 890 395	3 809 769

Which brick number
(a) has 210 thousands and 5 tens
(b) has 890 thousands and an odd hundreds digit
(c) is less than 2 million and has units digit 4
(d) is between 3 million and 4 million and has 7 hundreds
(e) has 809 thousands and a tens digit half of the units digit
(f) has more than 500 thousands and fewer than 3 units.

3

		Number made	Number still to be made
1	**(a)**	84 325	100
	(b)	193 400	100 000
	(c)	250 705	1000
	(d)	1 480 000	10 000

How many of each item will be made altogether?

2 How many of each item are **not** faulty?

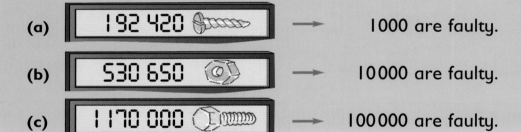

(a) 192 420   →   1000 are faulty.

(b) 530 650   →   10 000 are faulty.

(c) 1 170 000   →   100 000 are faulty.

3 Increase 1 358 247 by
   (a) one thousand   **(b)** one hundred   **(c)** ten thousand
   (d) ten   **(e)** one million   **(f)** one hundred thousand

4 Decrease 5 346 295 by
   (a) one million   **(b)** ten   **(c)** one hundred thousand
   (d) ten thousand   **(e)** one hundred   **(f)** one thousand.

5 **(a)** 269 450 + 1000   **(b)** 1 792 800 + 100 000
   (c) 3 604 240 − 10 000   **(d)** 10 230 020 − 1 000 000

1

Enter these numbers in your calculator.
Record each display **using numerals**.

(a) Fourteen thousand six hundred and twenty.

(b) One hundred and twenty-five thousand, eight hundred and nine.

(c) Three million, seven hundred and two thousand, four hundred.

(d) Ten million, three hundred and seventy thousand, eight hundred and eighty.

2 Start with  1 542 360 each time. Add

(a) 100   (b) 1000   (c) 10 000   (d) 1 000 000

3 Start with 12 673 458 each time. Subtract

(a) 1000   (b) 10   (c) 100 000   (d) 10 000 000

Check each answer with a calculator.

4 What has been **added** to change each display?

(a) 43 200 → 43 300   (b) 614 070 → 615 070

(c) 135 060 → 235 060   (d) 5 801 250 → 6 801 250

What has been **subtracted** to change each display?

(e) 94 150 → 94 140   (f) 205 739 → 204 739

(g) 4 240 000 → 3 240 000   (h) 568 127 → 558 127

5

1 Rob played games against the computer.
   Who had the higher score in each game?

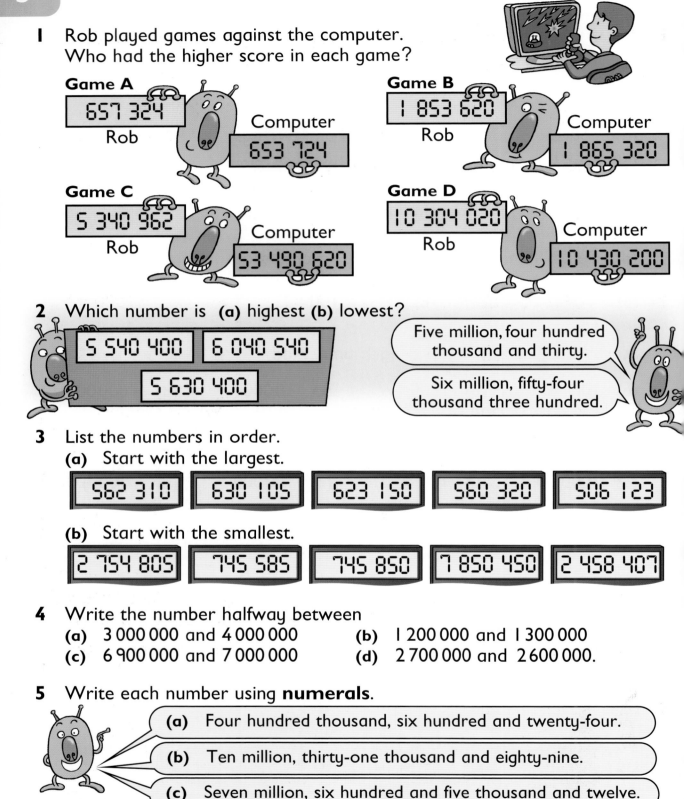

Game A
Rob 657 324
Computer 653 724

Game B
Rob 1 853 620
Computer 1 865 320

Game C
Rob 5 340 962
Computer 53 490 620

Game D
Rob 10 304 020
Computer 10 430 200

2 Which number is (a) highest (b) lowest?

5 540 400   6 040 540
      5 630 400

Five million, four hundred thousand and thirty.

Six million, fifty-four thousand three hundred.

3 List the numbers in order.
   (a) Start with the largest.

562 310   630 105   623 150   560 320   506 123

   (b) Start with the smallest.

2 754 805   745 585   745 850   7 850 450   2 458 407

4 Write the number halfway between
   (a) 3 000 000 and 4 000 000   (b) 1 200 000 and 1 300 000
   (c) 6 900 000 and 7 000 000   (d) 2 700 000 and 2 600 000.

5 Write each number using **numerals**.
   (a) Four hundred thousand, six hundred and twenty-four.
   (b) Ten million, thirty-one thousand and eighty-nine.
   (c) Seven million, six hundred and five thousand and twelve.

6 Write **in words**.
   (a)   53 000   (b)   175 002   (c)   120 713
   (d) 4 600 150   (e) 6 080 410   (f) 10 300 609

I These are the points scored for zapping each type of Space Invader.

10 points

100 points

1000 points

How many points are scored for zapping

(a) 23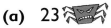
(b) 23
(c) 67
(d) 67

(e) 154
(f) 209
(g) 681
(h) 356

(i) 1300
(j) 7140
(k) 2065
(l) 1001 ?

2 (a) $18 \times 10 = \blacksquare$ (b) $62 \times 100 = \blacksquare$ (c) $7 \times 1000 = \blacksquare$

(d) $1000 \times 39 = \blacksquare$ (e) $100 \times 152 = \blacksquare$ (f) $1000 \times 5260 = \blacksquare$

(g) $96 \times \blacksquare = 960$ (h) $\blacksquare \times 14 = 14\,000$ (i) $\blacksquare \times 10 = 7340$

3 Find the cost of **one** of each game.

(a)

(b)

(c)

Toy World Orders		
Copies bought	Game	Total cost
10		£370
100		£10 400
1000		£43 000

4 (a) $620 \div 10 = \blacksquare$ (b) $1200 \div 100 = \blacksquare$ (c) $15\,000 \div 1000 = \blacksquare$

(d) $52\,000 \div 100 = \blacksquare$ (e) $70\,000 \div 1000 = \blacksquare$ (f) $5900 \div 10 = \blacksquare$

(g) $4700 \div \blacksquare = 470$ (h) $26\,000 \div \blacksquare = 260$ (i) $\blacksquare \div 1000 = 392$

5 Find the missing numbers.

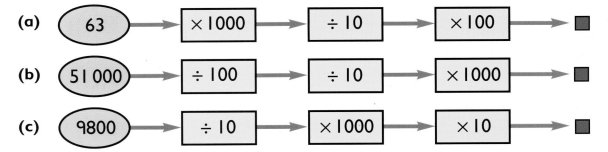

(a) 63 → ×1000 → ÷10 → ×100 → ■

(b) 51 000 → ÷100 → ÷10 → ×1000 → ■

(c) 9800 → ÷10 → ×1000 → ×10 → ■

Work in a group.

Challenge Card 1

(a) About how many pennies laid side by side are in a line one metre long?

(b) Approximately how many pennies would make a line one kilometre long?

(c) What would be the approximate **value** of one kilometre of pennies?

Challenge Card 2

(a) Choose a fiction book and count the number of words on one page.

(b) Estimate the total number of words in the book.

(c) Estimate how many phone numbers are in a telephone book.

Challenge Card 3

(a) Approximately how many crayons would have a total weight of one thousand kilograms?

(b) Estimate how many mathematics textbooks together weigh one thousand kilograms.

Challenge Card 4

Over 70 years, approximately how many

(a) bowls of cereal do you think you will eat

(b) loaves of bread do you think you will eat?

1. The graph shows the number of copies of some computer games sold by *Bug Byte* in one year.

To **the nearest thousand**, how many copies of each game were sold?

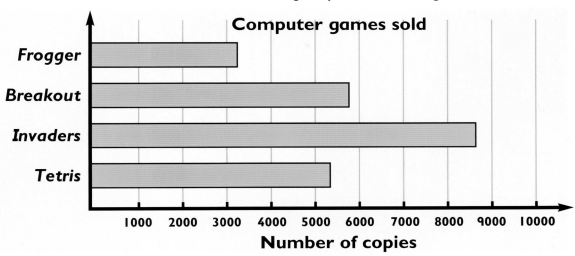

2 Round to **the nearest thousand**.

(a)	7358	**(b)**	12 196	**(c)**	29 803	**(d)**	50 099
(e)	19 583	**(f)**	61 758	**(g)**	132 052	**(h)**	554 454

3 Round to **the nearest hundred**.

(a)	259	**(b)**	534	**(c)**	2688	**(d)**	9149
(e)	34 769	**(f)**	21 081	**(g)**	143 208	**(h)**	320 851

4 This graph shows the amount of money spent **worldwide** on the games during the year.
To **the nearest million** pounds, find the total amount spent on each game.

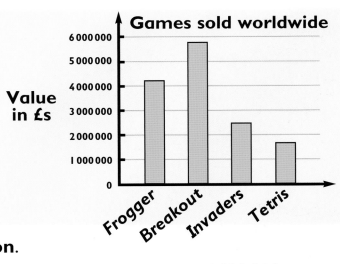

5 Round **to the nearest million**.

(a)	3 400 000	**(b)**	8 888 888	**(c)**	7 499 999
(d)	6 060 060	**(e)**	9 723 641	**(f)**	999 000
(g)	11 500 001	**(h)**	15 055 555	**(i)**	19 604 072

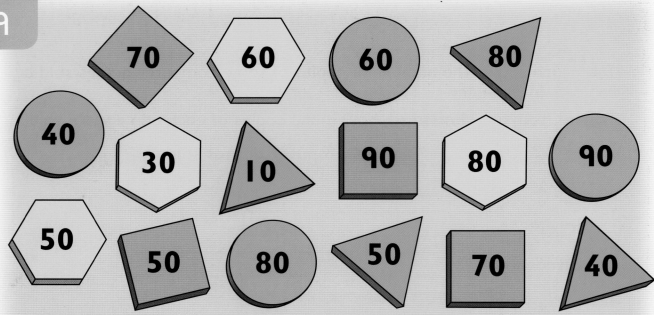

1 Find the total of the numbers on the
   (a) circles   **(b)** squares   **(c)** hexagons   **(d)** triangles.

2 **(a)** 20 + 90 + 30 + 50   **(b)** 80 + 40 + 20 + 80
   (c) 60 + 30 + 40 + 70 + 50   **(d)** 50 + 70 + 90 + 70 + 10

3 **(a)** 36 + 19 + 24 + 11   **(b)** 28 + 18 + 17 + 32   **(c)** 43 + 34 + 12 + 57
   (d) 22 + 84 + 16 + 51   **(e)** 93 + 62 + 25   **(f)** 84 + 43 + 69
   (g) 76 + 53 + 30 + 14   **(h)** 35 + 99 + 27 + 20   **(i)** 52 + 19 + 70 + 101
   (j) 44 + ■ + 66 = 200   **(k)** 87 + 35 + ■ = 190

4

I had 70 questions correct.

I answered 71 correctly.

I had 75 correct answers.

I had 77 correct.

How many questions altogether did these four children answer correctly?

5 **(a)** 62 + 63 + 61 + 60   **(b)** 58 + 51 + 56 + 53
   (c) 30 + 32 + 31 + 35 + 30   **(d)** 99 + 96 + 98 + 99 + 97

1. The table shows how many passengers travelled on some *Nippy Buses* routes one Saturday.

Destination	Arndale	Burness	Coalton	Deenby	Edenside	Fenmouth
Non-stop route	778	312	287	345	811	968
Stopping route	109	593	624	456	207	794

Round each number **to the nearest 100** to find the **approximate total** number of passengers who travelled on

- the non-stop **and** stopping routes to
(a) Arndale (b) Burness (c) Coalton (d) Deenby (e) Edenside (f) Fenmouth

- the non-stop routes to
(g) Arndale, Burness and Coalton   (h) Deenby, Edenside and Fenmouth

- the stopping routes to
(i) Arndale, Coalton and Deenby   (j) Burness, Edenside and Fenmouth.

2. The table shows how much altogether the passengers paid for tickets.

Destination	Arndale	Burness	Coalton	Deenby	Edenside	Fenmouth
Non-stop route	£312	£177	£324	£436	£241	£405
Stopping route	£107	£289	£463	£315	£58	£195

Round each amount **to the nearest £10** to find the **approximate total** cost of the tickets bought on

- the non-stop **and** stopping routes to
(a) Arndale (b) Burness (c) Coalton (d) Deenby (e) Edenside (f) Fenmouth

- the non-stop routes to
(g) Arndale, Deenby and Edenside   (h) Arndale, Burness and Fenmouth

- the stopping routes to
(i) Burness, Coalton and Edenside   (j) Coalton, Deenby and Fenmouth

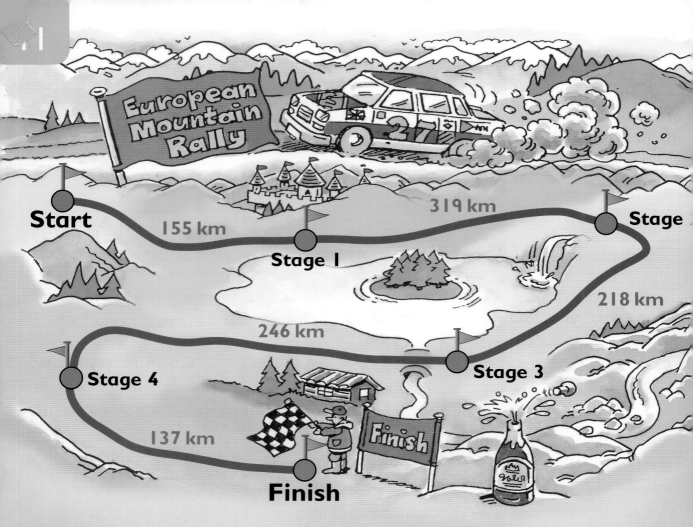

Start | 155 km | **Stage 1** | 319 km | **Stage**

246 km

218 km

Stage 4 | 137 km | **Finish** | **Stage 3**

European Mountain Rally

1 What is the distance between
  (a) the Start and Stage 2
  (c) Stage 2 and Stage 4
  (b) Stage 1 and Stage 3
  (c) Stage 3 and the Finish?

2 The Swedish car breaks down **halfway** between Stage 2 and Stage 3.
How far is the car from   **(a)** Stage 1   **(b)** Stage 4?

3 **(a)** 664 + 326   **(b)** 353 + 427   **(c)** 739 + 142   **(d)** 575 + 307
   (e) 436 + 146   **(f)** 428 + 267   **(g)** 848 + 128   **(h)** 244 + 438
   (i) 631 + 339   **(j)** 408 + 483   **(k)** 117 + 377   **(l)** 525 + 358

4 **(a)** 149 + ■ = 682   **(b)** 519 + ■ = 756   **(c)** ■ + 216 = 491

Jarrod's Department Store Shopper Survey

Number of shoppers entering store between:

8.00 am – 9.00 am	190
9.00 am – 10.00 am	243
10.00 am – 11.00 am	480
11.00 am – 12.00 noon	374
12.00 noon –1.00 pm	350
1.00 pm – 2.00 pm	568

1 How many shoppers entered Jarrod's between

(a) 8.00 am and 10.00 am

(b) 9.00 am and 11.00 am

(c) 10.00 am and 12.00 noon

(d) 11.00 am and 1.00 pm

(e) 12.00 noon and 2.00 pm?

2

(a) 290 + 560

(b) 464 + 470

(c) 530 + 186

(d) 663 + 263

(e) 557 + 282

(f) 182 + 685

(g) 493 + 272

(h) 275 + 341

(i) 294 + 255

(j) 381 + 166

(k) 694 + 184

(l) 177 + 732

3

(a) $193 + \blacksquare = 753$

(b) $770 + \blacksquare = 945$

(c) $\blacksquare + 453 = 909$

4 The number of shoppers entering Jarrod's

- between 2.00 pm and 3.00 pm was **twice** as many as between 8.00 am and 9.00 am
- between 3.00 pm and 4.00 pm was **half** as many as between 10.00 am and 11.00 am.

How many shoppers entered Jarrod's between 2.00 pm and 4.00 pm?

TRAVEL SAVE

Adventure Holidays

Surfing in Australia *£840*

Trekking in Nepal *£704*

Cycling in Ireland *£222*

Diving in the Caribbean *£931*

Hang-gliding in Hawaii *£955*

Canoeing in Canada *£513*

1 How much altogether do these holidays cost?

- (a) Surfing and Trekking
- (b) Cycling and Surfing
- (c) Hang-gliding and Canoeing
- (d) Trekking and Hang-gliding
- (e) Diving and Surfing
- (f) Canoeing and Trekking
- (g) Trekking and Diving
- (h) Hang-gliding and Cycling
- (i) Canoeing and Diving
- (j) Surfing and Canoeing

2
- (a) 360 + 830
- (b) 408 + 680
- (c) 770 + 707
- (d) 154 + 924
- (e) 635 + 853
- (f) 517 + 661
- (g) 732 + 527
- (h) 444 + 814
- (i) 650 + ■ = 1170
- (j) ■ + 380 = 1290
- (k) 827 + ■ = 1648

3

TRAVEL SAVE last minute bargains!

For all Adventure Holidays
- take £29 off prices more than £600
- take £15 off prices less than £600.

Find the total **bargain price** of the Adventure Holidays.

- (a) Diving and Cycling
- (b) Surfing and Canoeing

Supplier	Amount
Brookes	£5600
Afkar	£2300
Minvac	£4700
Scotvale	£1100
Quikfix	£3200

1 Susan is the manager at *Sofashop*. She pays the amounts shown in the table to suppliers. What is the total amount paid to
(a) *Scotvale* and *Quikfix* (b) *Quikfix* and *Minvas*
(c) *Afkar* and *Brookes* (d) *Minvac* and *Scotvale*
(e) *Scotvale* and *Afkar* (f) *Quikfix* and *Brookes*?

2 (a) $1700 + 6300 = \blacksquare$ (b) $2800 + 1500 = \blacksquare$ (c) $5800 + 2600 = \blacksquare$

(d) $6500 + 1900 = \blacksquare$ (e) $1600 + \blacksquare = 5500$ (f) $\blacksquare + 6600 = 9500$

3 Each day, Susan goes to the bank with *Sofashop's* takings.

Day	Takings
Monday	£9100
Tuesday	£5300
Wednesday	£4500
Thursday	£8200
Friday	£7600
Saturday	£7300

What were the total takings on
(a) Monday and Tuesday (b) Wednesday and Thursday
(c) Friday and Saturday (d) Tuesday and Thursday
(e) Monday and Friday (f) Wednesday and Saturday?

4 (a) $7200 + 4800 = \blacksquare$ (b) $8400 + 6700 = \blacksquare$ (c) $9400 + 9800 = \blacksquare$

(d) $8500 + 2700 = \blacksquare$ (e) $3300 + \blacksquare = 13200$ (f) $\blacksquare + 3800 = 10200$

class ✓

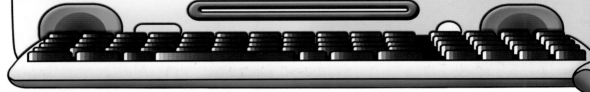

Website	Number of visitors		
	Day 1	Day 2	Day 3
music4u.co	2634	2352	5637
sportsnews.co	3507	2431	4468
gameszone.co	6851	3043	2556
fashion.co	4062	1935	7043
starsigns.co	1826	5142	3737
freebie.co	5640	4255	4324

1 How many visitors altogether did each website have on

(a) Day 1 and Day 2   (b) Day 2 and Day 3?

2

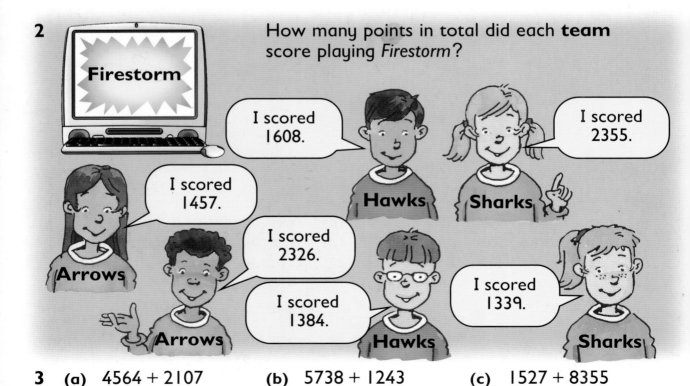

How many points in total did each **team** score playing *Firestorm*?

Firestorm

I scored 1608. — Hawks

I scored 2355. — Sharks

I scored 1457. — Arrows

I scored 2326. I scored 1384. — Arrows

I scored 1384. — Hawks

I scored 1339. — Sharks

3 (a) 4564 + 2107   (b) 5738 + 1243   (c) 1527 + 8355

Swift £7687

Gull £6599

Puffin £5628

Shark £1283

Marlin £1346

Dolphin £1479

1 Find the total cost of

(a) *Marlin* and *Puffin*   (b) *Shark* and *Gull*   (c) *Puffin* and *Shark*

(d) *Dolphin* and *Gull*   (e) *Swift* and *Dolphin*   (f) *Marlin* and *Swift*.

2

S.S. Storm   S.S. Tempest   S.S. Spray   S.S. Coral

Liner	Miles Cruised		
	July	August	September
S.S. Storm	5 257	4328	5973
S.S. Tempest	6046	3185	6839
S.S. Spray	5354	4546	6965
S.S. Coral	5367	3857	9463

How many miles altogether did each liner cruise in

(a) July **and** August   (b) August **and** September?

3 (a) 8545 + 6408   (b) 2619 + 9732   (c) 4208 + 7494

   (d) 4236 + 7895   (e) 6857 + 8584   (f) 5672 + 7938

1 Find each child's total score.

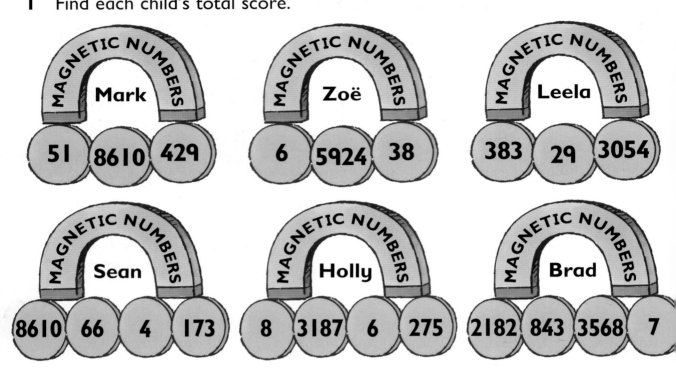

Mark: 51 8610 429

Zoë: 6 5924 38

Leela: 383 29 3054

Sean: 8610 66 4 173

Holly: 8 3187 6 275

Brad: 2182 843 3568 7

2 Find each team's total score.

TEAM A: 486 7 531 2598 42

TEAM B: 1258 649 55 3 4857

TEAM C: 8 3074 2296 63 562

3 (a) 42 + 3509 + 8 + 176 + 55
(b) 5 + 8027 + 649 + 31 + 234
(c) 1357 + 4 + 45 + 8 + 606
(d) 1096 + 833 + 7 + 48 + 612
(e) 45 + 3 + 5064 + 93 + 8708
(f) 9 + 842 + 7070 + 56 + 3413

4 (a) 6 + 8135 + ■ + 364 = 8600
(b) 72 + ■ + 6058 + 4 = 6240

done in class

PICK 'N' MIX

6	5754	739	13 146	82
36	3	6108	537	12 908
12 507	72	8	5956	459
210	11 365	54	9	7835
8879	893	13 077	61	5

1 **Estimate** first, then check using a calculator.

(a) Which **row** has the greatest total?

(b) Which **column** has the smallest total?

2 Add the numbers in five **differently-coloured** boxes each time.

(a) What is the smallest possible total?

(b) What is the largest possible total?

3 Which two numbers have a sum of 13 200?

4 Make a total of 999 by adding two numbers in blue boxes and one in a red box.

5 Choose five numbers, each from a differently-coloured box. Find **all** the totals that can be made by adding **four** of the numbers at a time.

6 Which three numbers in green boxes add to give a total where all of the digits are even?

dene by Ariasun

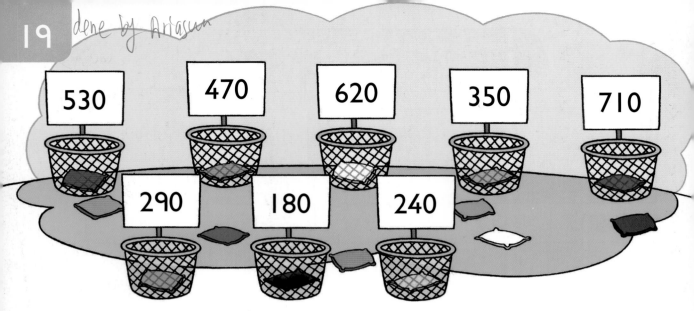

1 Find the difference between the number of points scored by

   (a) the red and yellow bean bags
   (b) the green and blue bean bags
   (c) the white and orange bean bags
   (d) the black and brown bean bags.

2 **(a)** 550 – 260 = ■   **(b)** 640 – 470 = ■   **(c)** 420 – 180 = ■
   (d) 930 – 370 = ■   **(e)** 810 – 230 = ■   **(f)** 740 – 560 = ■
   (g) 730 – ■ = 380   **(h)** ■ – 540 = 290   **(i)** 860 – ■ = 570

3

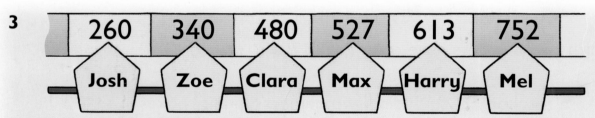

Find the difference between the scores of

   (a) Max and Zoe   **(b)** Josh and Harry   **(c)** Clara and Mel
   (d) Max and Clara   **(e)** Harry and Zoe   **(f)** Mel and Josh.

4 **(a)** 324 – 160   **(b)** 936 – 580   **(c)** 875 – 690   **(d)** 705 – 420
   (e) 443 – 150   **(f)** 768 – 380   **(g)** 821 – 270   **(h)** 922 – 460
   (i) 566 – 290   **(j)** 919 – 330   **(k)** 608 – 440   **(l)** 331 – 180

5 **(a)** 736 – ■ = 556   **(b)** 951 – ■ = 261   **(c)** 611 – ■ = 281
   (d) ■ – 120 = 184   **(e)** ■ – 360 = 267   **(f)** ■ – 180 = 674

£610

£450

£366

£187 Empire 6d

£295

£373

£560

£840

I Find the difference between the value of

(a) the camera and the vase   (b) the coin and the stamp
(c) the clock and the ring   (d) the book and the sword
(e) the stamp and the clock   (f) the camera and the book
(g) the sword and the vase   (h) the ring and the coin.

2 (a) 820 – 442   (b) 730 – 564   (c) 550 – 178   (d) 910 – 581
(e) 670 – 282   (f) 740 – 497   (g) 830 – 275   (h) 860 – 586
(i) 630 – 193   (j) 650 – 464   (k) 710 – 238   (l) 940 – 679

3

243 pages

920 pages

510 pages

HISTORY OF THE WORLD
470 pages

(a) The red book has 286 pages with pictures.
How many pages do not have pictures?

(b) How many more pages has the green book than the yellow book?

(c) Marvin has 127 pages of the brown book still to read.
How many pages has he read?

(d) Susie has read 94 pages of the yellow book.
Amy has read double that number of pages of the green book.
How many pages has Amy still to read?

TRAVEL SAVE

BARGAIN BREAKS

CYPRUS £674   MAJORCA £345   CRETE £591   TURKEY £117

FLORIDA £883   IBIZA £268   CORFU £462   MENORCA £236

1 Find the difference between the cost of breaks to

(a) Crete and Ibiza
(b) Cyprus and Menorca
(c) Florida and Majorca
(d) Corfu and Turkey
(e) Menorca and Crete
(f) Ibiza and Florida
(g) Majorca and Cyprus
(h) Turkey and Majorca.

2
(a) 892 – 546   (b) 747 – 428   (c) 971 – 354   (d) 665 – 138
(e) 995 – 759   (f) 676 – 427   (g) 781 – 563   (h) 522 – 305
(i) 764 – 227   (j) 862 – 349   (k) 391 – 165   (l) 273 – 146

3

Palm Beach Hotel 456 rooms altogether

Coral View Hotel 157 rooms are occupied

Hotel Tropica 214 rooms are vacant

(a) *Palm Beach Hotel* has 239 rooms vacant. How many rooms are occupied?

(b) *Coral View Hotel* has 383 rooms altogether. How many are vacant?

(c) *Hotel Tropica* has 552 rooms altogether. How many are occupied?

Barndale Borough Council
Village Population Survey

Village	Total population	Number of people under 25 years old
Firth	3956	
Boulter	2894	703
Ainley	9437	661
Sorn	7568	2015
Gilton	9985	1352
Rebway	6722	3124
		1220

1 How many people in each village are **not** under 25 years old?

2
(a) 8341 – 5031
(b) 1348 – 1036
(c) 5666 – 2222
(d) 9876 – 8765
(e) 3000 – 1001
(f) 4950 – 3145

3 The number of people aged 60 or over who live in each village is:
- Firth 538
- Boulter 745
- Ainley 3119
- Sorn 2329
- Gilton 1856
- Rebway 2607.

How many people in each village are **less than** 60 years old?

Sandya **Andrew** **Mollie**

1 What is the difference between the weights guessed by

(a) Andrew and Sandya   (b) Mollie and Sandya
(c) William and Andrew   (d) Mollie and William
(e) Andrew and Mollie   (f) Sandya and William?

2 (a) 9834 – 5467   (b) 6672 – 2945   (c) 7426 – 3581
(d) 8313 – 4759   (e) 4153 – 1297   (f) 5060 – 2179

3

The large cake weighs 2450 g and the small cake weighs 235 g.
How much heavier is the large cake?

4 (a) 3649 – 217   (b) 4385 – 92   (c) 7153 – 826
(d) 6734 – 78   (e) 8461 – 992   (f) 5003 – 685

5 The medium cake is 1127 g heavier than the small cake.
What is the difference between the weights of the **large** cake and the
medium cake?

1 The difference between two multiples of 10 is 330.
Their total is 710.
What are the two numbers?

2 Copy and complete each subtraction chain.

(a) 8000 - 2700 → ■ - 1500 → ■ - 2250 → ■ - 600 → ■ - 384 → ■

(b) 6000 - 3524 → ■ - 1258 → ■ - 400 → ■ - 209 → ■ - 440 → ■

3

$$8036 - 1275 = 6761$$

Use the subtraction story to find:

(a) 8036 - 6760   (b) 6761 + 1271   (c) 8000 - 6761

(d) 1280 + 6761   (e) 8036 - 1250   (f) 8030 - 1270

4 List pairs of these numbers which have a difference of 79.

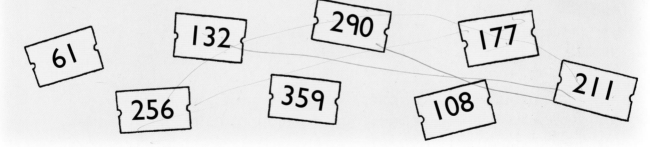

61   132   290   177   256   359   108   211

5 Find the missing numbers.

(a) $803\,516 - ■ = 783\,929$ (b) $■ - 15\,889 = 77\,777$

6 Find the missing digits.

(a) $67■5 - △306 = 1409$ (b) $93\,26■ - 4△◇51 = 46\,014$

| Happytot £24 | Robotot £33 | Furrytot £27 | Nosytot £46 |

1 Find the cost of

(a) 4 Happytots (b) 2 Furrytots (c) 6 Nosytots
(d) 3 Robotots   (e) 5 Happytots (f) 3 Furrytots
(g) 8 Nosytots   (h) 7 Furrytots (i) 5 Robotots

2 (a) 3×29 (b) 2×67 (c) 76×5 (d) 89×4
(e) 6×38 (f) 46×7 (g) 65×8 (h) 9×18

3

| 4 Happytots | 6 Furrytots | 8 Robotots |

How many

(a) Happytots are in 45 boxes   (b) Furrytots are in 27 boxes
(c) Robotots are in 68 boxes   (d) Happytots are in 76 boxes
(e) Furrytots are in 34 boxes   (f) Robotots are in 69 boxes?

4 Seven children each have a complete collection of 36 Cybertots. How many Cybertots do they have altogether?

5 A battery pack for a Cybertot costs £9. What is the cost of 53 battery packs?

1
(a) 5×34 (b) 62×5 (c) 35×18 (d) 16×45
(e) 35×14 (f) 54×5 (g) 14×25 (h) 25×16

2
(a) Multiply 5 by 44.   (b) 18 times 45
(c) 5 multiplied by 76   (d) Multiply 14 by 15.

3 How many sheets are there in
(a) 12 notepads   (b) 18 notepads?

15 sheets

4 How many pencils are there in
(a) 35 packets   (b) 45 packets?

12 pencils

5
(a) 16×13 (b) 18×17 (c) 14×33 (d) 12×37
(e) 27×14 (f) 44×12 (g) 31×16 (h) 18×42

6 How many
(a) books are in 12 boxes
(b) comics are in 18 boxes?

22 books

29 comics

7
(a) 50×26 (b) 50×38 (c) 42×50 (d) 54×50
(e) 25×24 (f) 25×36 (g) 48×25 (h) 56×25

8 Which pair of numbers gives a product of
(a) 800   (b) 1300?

| 25 | 26 | 32 | 50 | 52 |

1 Copy and complete each example **to multiply by 50**.

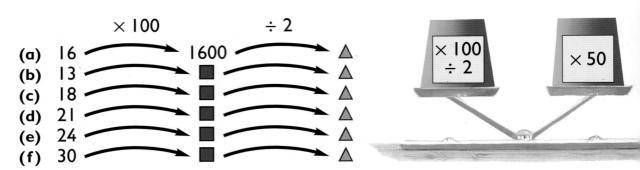

$\times 100$ $\div 2$

(a) 16 ⟶ 1600 ⟶ △
(b) 13 ⟶ ■ ⟶ △
(c) 18 ⟶ ■ ⟶ △
(d) 21 ⟶ ■ ⟶ △
(e) 24 ⟶ ■ ⟶ △
(f) 30 ⟶ ■ ⟶ △

2 Multiply each number by 50.

(a) 28   (b) 22   (c) 15   (d) 36   (e) 44   (f) 67

3 (a) $50 \times \blacksquare = 2000$ (b) $\blacksquare \times 50 = 3800$ (c) $50 \times \blacksquare = 4950$

4 Copy and complete this doubles table for 25.

$1 \times 25 = \blacksquare$
$2 \times 25 = \blacksquare$
$4 \times 25 = \blacksquare$
$8 \times 25 = \blacksquare$

5 Use your doubles table to find the missing numbers.

(a) $(1 \times 25) + (8 \times 25) = \blacksquare$ (b) $(2 \times 25) + (4 \times 25) = \blacksquare$
(c) $(4 \times 25) + (1 \times 25) = \blacksquare$ (d) $(8 \times 25) + (2 \times 25) = \blacksquare$
(e) $(8 \times 25) - (1 \times 25) = \blacksquare$ (f) $(4 \times 25) - (1 \times 25) = \blacksquare$

6 (a) 11×25 (b) 13×25 (c) 15×25 (d) 20×25
   (e) 25×18 (f) 48×25 (g) 25×42 (h) 25×34

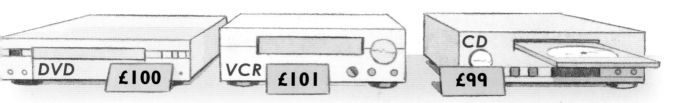

1 How much does it cost to buy
   (a) • 14 DVD players   • 14 VCRs   • 14 CD players
   (b) • 23 DVD players   • 23 VCRs   • 23 CD players?

2 (a) 100 × 34   (b) 101 × 17   (c) 99 × 16
   (d) 101 × 28   (e) 100 × 19   (f) 101 × 31
   (g) 99 × 34   (h) 100 × 26   (i) 99 × 28

3

   (a) Find the cost of
      • 13 blue radios   • 13 green radios   • 13 red radios
   (b) Repeat to find the cost of 24 radios in each colour.
   (c) Repeat for 19 radios.

4 (a) 50 × 18   (b) 51 × 12   (c) 49 × 26
   (d) 49 × 17   (e) 50 × 21   (f) 51 × 27

5 What is the total cost of
   (a) 49 mobile phones
   (b) 50 headphones
   (c) 46 games consoles
   (d) 49 headphones
   (e) 51 mobile phones
   (f) 29 minidisc players?

Bostock Ballet

	Grand Circle	Front Stalls	Back Stalls
Adult	£28	£23	£15
Child	£21	£17	£12

1 How much does it cost to buy

   (a) 7 adult tickets in the Grand Circle

   (b) 9 child tickets in the Front Stalls

   (c) 14 adult tickets in the Back Stalls

   (d) 6 adult tickets and 4 child tickets in the Front Stalls

   (e) 8 adult tickets and 5 child tickets in the Grand Circle

   (f) 12 adult tickets and 24 child tickets in the Back Stalls?

2 Blythwood School orders 58 child tickets and 7 adult tickets for the Wednesday matinee.

How much does this cost altogether?

> **Bostock Ballet**
> Wednesday matinee
> All seats
> Adult £13 Child £6

3

	Grand Circle	Back Stalls	Front Stalls
Number of rows	13	34	17
Number of seats in a row	50	49	51

How many seats are there in the

   (a) Grand Circle   **(b)** Front Stalls   **(c)** Back Stalls?

4 These items were sold during an interval.

18 ◁ 45 p   14 ◁ 32 p   49 ◁ 58p   25 ◁ 27 p

How much was spent altogether?

Travelsave
Luxury Holidays

Egypt	Australia	Mexico	Kenya

adult £2517	adult £7018	adult £4356	adult £2976
child £1259	child £3509	child £2178	child £1488

China	Alaska	India	Brazil

adult £5568	adult £7466	adult £5472	adult £9630
child £2784	child £3733	child £2736	child £4815

1 Find the total cost of each holiday.

- **(a)** 7 adults to Kenya
- **(b)** 3 adults to Australia
- **(c)** 5 adults to Mexico
- **(d)** 2 adults to Egypt
- **(e)** 9 adults to India
- **(f)** 6 adults to Alaska
- **(g)** 4 adults to China
- **(h)** 8 adults to Brazil

2 Find the total cost of each holiday.

- **(a)** 2 adults and 5 children to India
- **(b)** 3 adults and 7 children to Brazil
- **(c)** 4 adults and 8 children to Australia
- **(d)** 6 adults and 9 children to Kenya

3 The Blake family won a luxury holiday.
The value of the holiday was £19 152.
Which country did they visit?

1 Each visit to the Bell family's country cottage involves a round trip of 78 miles.
One year, they make 43 visits.

How many miles do they travel altogether?

2 A delicatessen orders 82 Dutch cheeses which cost 26 Euros each.

What is the total cost, in Euros, of the cheeses?

3 An internet service allows each non-member 45 minutes of free time on-line.

How many minutes altogether of free time would 81 non-members be allowed?

4

I saved 75p a week for 32 weeks.

I saved 65p a week for 37 weeks.

Salim

Briony

Who saved more money?

5 Each edition of *Music Crazy* contains 24 pages.

How many pages are there in 64 editions?

6
(a) 18×57	(b) 33×46	(c) 54×89	(d) 92×14
(e) 88×44	(f) 29×76	(g) 31×74	(h) 42×63
(i) 19×91	(j) 58×59	(k) 86×86	(l) 93×97

Topside Council
Homes for rent

Homes for rent	Rent per month
Flat	£197
Terraced house	£219
Semi - detached house	£248
Small detached house	£275
Large detached house	£313

1 How much rent should Topside Council collect from each group of homes in
- one month   • one year?

(a) 48 flats
(b) 36 terraced houses
(c) 32 semi-detached houses
(d) 28 small detached houses
(e) 21 large detached houses

2 Topside Council decides to build a range of new homes on some empty land.
(a) Which of these options would gather more rent in **one year**?
(b) How much more?

Option One
6	blocks of 6 flats
24	terraced houses
32	semi - detached houses
18	small detached houses

Option Two
4	blocks of 8 flats
19	semi - detached houses
27	small detached houses
26	large detached houses

33

1 Divide equally.

    (a) 42 mountain bikes ⟶ 6 racks   **(b)** 48 skateboards ⟶ 8 boxes
    (c) 40 basketballs ⟶ 8 nets   **(d)** 81 golf clubs ⟶ 9 bags
    (e) 50 rollerblades ⟶ 10 cases   **(f)** 28 snooker cues ⟶ 7 tables

2 **(a)** $49 \div 7$ **(b)** $40 \div 4$ **(c)** $70 \div 7$ **(d)** $45 \div 9$ **(e)** $56 \div 8$ **(f)** $54 \div 6$
   (g) $72 \div 8$ **(h)** $27 \div 9$ **(i)** $36 \div 9$ **(j)** $35 \div 7$ **(k)** $100 \div 10$ **(l)** $63 \div 7$

3 Find the missing numbers.

    (a) $\dfrac{21}{\square} = 7$ **(b)** $\dfrac{\square}{9} = 8$ **(c)** $\dfrac{30}{\square} = 5$ **(d)** $\dfrac{\square}{6} = 8$ **(e)** $\dfrac{60}{\square} = 10$

    (f) $\dfrac{\square}{8} = 4$ **(g)** $\dfrac{24}{\square} = 3$ **(h)** $\dfrac{\square}{4} = 4$ **(i)** $\dfrac{36}{\square} = 6$ **(j)** $\dfrac{\square}{10} = 9$

4 Divide the equipment equally among the teams.
   How many items are given to each team and how many are left over?

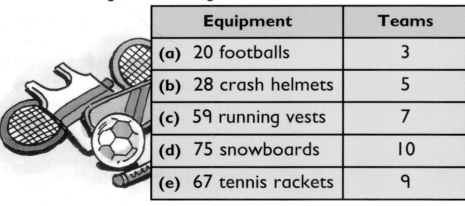

Equipment	Teams
(a) 20 footballs	3
(b) 28 crash helmets	5
(c) 59 running vests	7
(d) 75 snowboards	10
(e) 67 tennis rackets	9

5 **(a)** $80 \div 9 = \blacksquare$ **(b)** $47 \div 7 = \blacksquare$ **(c)** $86 \div 10 = \blacksquare$ **(d)** $19 \div 2 = \blacksquare$
   (e) $45 \div 6 = \blacksquare$ **(f)** $29 \div 9 = \blacksquare$ **(g)** $53 \div 5 = \blacksquare$ **(h)** $7 \div 8 = \blacksquare$
   (i) $\frac{1}{6}$ of $62 = \blacksquare$ **(j)** $\frac{1}{3}$ of $26 = \blacksquare$ **(k)** $\frac{1}{8}$ of $86 = \blacksquare$ **(l)** $\frac{1}{7}$ of $20 = \blacksquare$

6   One eighth of the practice golf balls are *Superflite*.
    One seventh of the rest are *Fairway*.
    How many golf balls are **not** *Superflite*
    or *Fairway*?

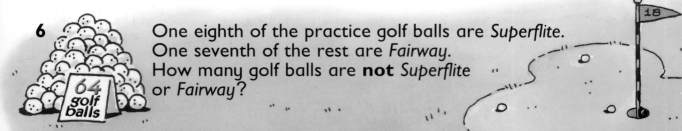

64 golf balls

ASHWAY LEISURE CENTRE
Sponsored Sports Week

1 The players in each team raised an equal amount of money.

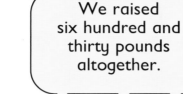

We raised a total of two hundred and forty pounds.

We raised six hundred and thirty pounds altogether.

Our total was eight hundred and ten pounds.

How much money was raised by each player in

(a) the red team   **(b)** the blue team   **(c)** the green team?

2
(a) $320 \div 8 = \blacksquare$ **(b)** $480 \div 6 = \blacksquare$ **(c)** $270 \div 3 = \blacksquare$ **(d)** $540 \div 9 = \blacksquare$
(e) $360 \div 4 = \blacksquare$ **(f)** $450 \div 5 = \blacksquare$ **(g)** $490 \div 7 = \blacksquare$ **(h)** $560 \div 8 = \blacksquare$
(i) $280 \div \blacksquare = 40$ **(j)** $720 \div \blacksquare = 80$ **(k)** $640 \div \blacksquare = 80$ **(l)** $210 \div \blacksquare = 70$

3 The cyclists in each team completed an equal number of laps.
How many laps did each cycle?

(a) Team total: 78 laps   **(b)** Team total: 108 laps   **(c)** Team total: 105 laps   **(d)** Team total: 104 laps

4
(a) $52 \div 4$ **(b)** $91 \div 7$ **(c)** $60 \div 5$ **(d)** $39 \div 3$ **(e)** $99 \div 9$ **(f)** $84 \div 6$
(g) $96 \div 8$ **(h)** $57 \div 3$ **(i)** $72 \div 6$ **(j)** $68 \div 4$ **(k)** $75 \div 5$ **(l)** $117 \div 9$

5
(a) $848 \div 4$ **(b)** $763 \div 7$ **(c)** $819 \div 9$ **(d)** $486 \div 6$ **(e)** $159 \div 3$
(f) $455 \div 5$ **(g)** $832 \div 8$ **(h)** $567 \div 7$ **(i)** $624 \div 6$ **(j)** $404 \div 4$

1 Joe Bloggs' election publicity items
are shared equally among boxes.
How many items are in each box?

(a) 4260
stickers

in 5 boxes

(b) 2892
badges

in 3 boxes

(c) 3672
posters

in 9 boxes

(d) 5724
leaflets

in 6 boxes

(e) 7032
letters

in 8 boxes

2 **(a)** $6252 \div 4$ **(b)** $7945 \div 7$ **(c)** $8758 \div 2$ **(d)** $9837 \div 9$
   (e) $9132 \div 6$ **(f)** $8256 \div 4$ **(g)** $9072 \div 7$ **(h)** $7005 \div 5$

3 Voting papers are shared equally among vote counters.
How many papers does each counter receive and how many
are left over?

(a)

5027
voting papers

6 counters

(b)

3853
voting papers

8 counters

(c)

2200
voting papers

3 counters

4 **(a)** $3575 \div 4$ **(b)** $1986 \div 5$ **(c)** $4903 \div 3$ **(d)** $3157 \div 2$
   (e) $9041 \div 7$ **(f)** $8200 \div 8$ **(g)** $9119 \div 9$ **(h)** $6006 \div 5$

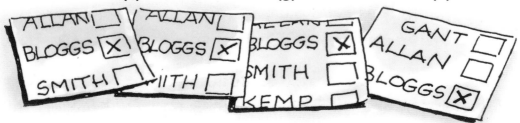

Zipways Security

I The badges show each security guard's number.

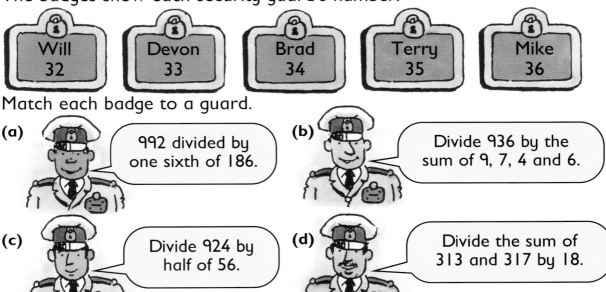

Will	Devon	Brad	Terry	Mike
32	33	34	35	36

Match each badge to a guard.

(a) 992 divided by one sixth of 186.

(b) Divide 936 by the sum of 9, 7, 4 and 6.

(c) Divide 924 by half of 56.

(d) Divide the sum of 313 and 317 by 18.

2 Write a division clue for the remaining security guard's badge number.

3

848 gold bars are shared equally among 16 safes.
How many bars are there in 12 of these safes?

Zipways Transport

4

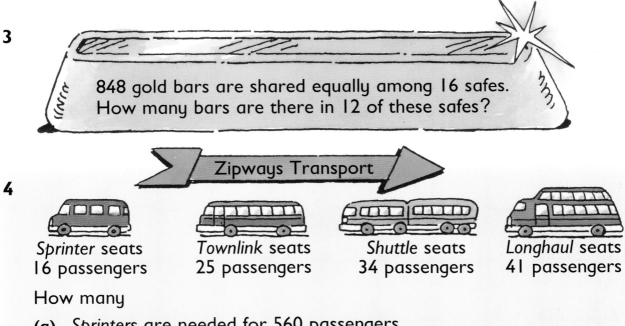

Sprinter seats 16 passengers

Townlink seats 25 passengers

Shuttle seats 34 passengers

Longhaul seats 41 passengers

How many

(a) *Sprinters* are needed for 560 passengers
(b) *Townlinks* are needed for 965 passengers
(c) *Shuttles* are needed for 918 passengers
(d) *Longhauls* are needed for 887 passengers?

5 Each *Zipways* plane has seats for 32 passengers.
How many planes would be needed to carry 760 passengers?

1 Write each child's number sequence.

(a)

Start at 24. Count on in 6s to 96.

(b)

Start at 3. Count on in 8s to 67.

(c)

Start at 72. Count back in 7s to 9.

(d)

Start at 94. Count back in 11s to 6.

(e)

Start at 42. Count on in 9s to 96.

(f)

Start at 257. Count back in 25s to 7.

2

128, 64, 32, 16, 8, 4, 2, 1

The rule for my number sequence is **divide by 2** each time.

Copy each sequence and write the next four numbers.
Write the rule for each sequence.

(a) 10, 25, 40, 55, ...   **(b)** 5, 12, 19, 26, ...
(c) 79, 73, 67, 61, ...   **(d)** 263, 242, 221, 200, ...
(e) 25, 44, 63, 82, ...   **(f)** 92, 84, 76, 68, ...
(g) 10, 9·5, 9, 8·5, ...   **(h)** 1, 2, 4, 8, ...

3 Copy and complete each number sequence and write the rule.

(a) 5, 16, 27, ■, ■, 60   **(b)** 79, 64, 49, ■, ■, 4
(c) 13, 38, 63, ■, ■, 138   **(d)** 122, ■, ■, 65, 46, 27
(e) ■, 31, 50, ■, 88, 107   **(f)** 3, 6, 12, 24, ■, ■

1 Which of the door numbers are

   (a) square numbers

   (b) square **and** even

   (c) odd **and not** square?

2 **(a)** List the first twelve square numbers.

   (b) Calculate each square number from 13^2 to 20^2.

3 Use your answers to question **2.**

   (a) Find a pair of square numbers with a total of ● 65 ● 250.

   (b) Find pairs of square numbers with a total which is also
      a square number.

4

Bill the builder lays **square** patios using identical square slabs.

   (a) How many slabs lie along each edge of a patio with
      ● 25 slabs   ● 81 slabs ?

   (b) Find the number of slabs on each edge of a patio with
      ● 961 slabs   ● 2704 slabs.

5 **(a)** Copy this pattern and extend
      it for two more rows.

$$2^2 - 1^2 = 4 - 1 = 3 = 2+1$$
$$3^2 - 2^2 = 9 - 4 = 5 = 3+2$$
$$4^2 - 3^2 = 16 - 9 = 7 = 4+3$$

   (b) **Without** extending the pattern further, find mentally
      ● $9^2 - 8^2$ ● $10^2 - 9^2$

   (c) Copy and complete Bill's rule.

> The difference between the squares of two
> consecutive whole numbers is equal to …

1 (a) Grandpa's age is an even
       number **between** 50 and 60.
       What age could he be?
   (b) Jenny's age is an odd
       number between 5 and 15.
       What age could she be?

2

Find the product of the numbers on these birthday badges.

   (a) red and blue   (b) yellow and green   (c) orange and purple
   (d) orange and yellow (e) red and purple   (f) green and blue

3 (a) In question **2**, what type of number is   • each badge number
                                                    • each product?

   (b) What is true about the product of two even numbers?

4 Find the product of the numbers on each pair of birthday cards.

   (a)   (b)   (c)

   (d)   (e)   (f)

5 What is true about the product of two odd numbers?

6 Find out about the product
   of an odd and an even number.
   Write about what you find.

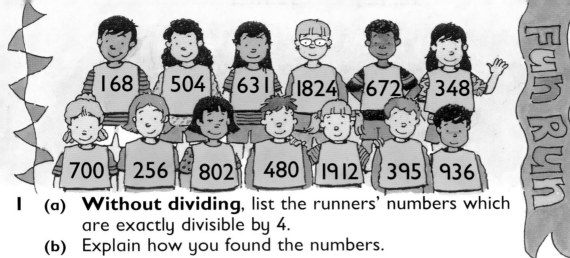

1 (a) **Without dividing**, list the runners' numbers which are exactly divisible by 4.

(b) Explain how you found the numbers.

2 (a) Which of the runners' numbers are exactly divisible by 8?

(b) Copy and complete.

Numbers exactly divisible by 8	168							
Half of the number	84							
Is the half exactly divisible by 4?	Yes							

(c) How can you tell, without dividing, that a number is exactly divisible by 8?

3

96	246	303	67	648	810	951

293	534	174	429	342	1668	785

(a) **Without dividing**, list the vest numbers which are exactly divisible by 3.

(b) Explain how you found the numbers.

4 (a) List the vest numbers which are exactly divisible by 6.

(b) Check, without dividing, that what Rosa says about these numbers is true.

> Each number is even...
> ...and is exactly divisible by 3.

(c) How can you tell, without dividing, that a number is exactly divisible by 6?

5 Without dividing, list the numbers from 430 to 440 which are

(a) exactly divisible by 8

(b) **not** exactly divisible by 6.

41

1 List the table numbers which are • multiples of 4 • multiples of 5.

2 **(a)** List the first ten • multiples of 7 • multiples of 9.
(b) Which multiples of 7 in part **(a)** are exactly divisible by 3?
(c) Which multiples of 9 in part **(a)** are exactly divisible by 4?

3 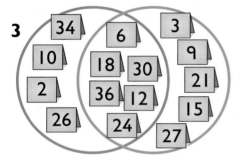 **(a)** What type of numbers are in
• the red circle • the green circle?
(b) List, in order, the numbers that are in **both** the red **and** the green circles.
(c) Describe these numbers in **two** different ways.

4 **(a)** List the first twenty • multiples of 2 • multiples of 5.
(b) List the numbers in part **(a)** that are multiples of **both** 2 **and** 5.
(c) Which is the smallest number that is a **common** multiple of 2 and 5?

5 Write the smallest number that is a common multiple of
(a) 2 and 7 **(b)** 6 and 5 **(c)** 3 and 8 **(d)** 7 and 5
(e) 4 and 10 **(f)** 12 and 8 **(g)** 6 and 15 **(h)** 9 and 36

6 **(a)** What colour is the 60th square in this pattern?

▢▢▢▢▢▢▢▢▢▢▢▢▢▢▢▢▢▢▢ . . .

(b) What is the position in the pattern of the 22nd yellow square?

7 **(a)** What colour is the 67th square in this pattern?

▢▢▢▢▢▢▢▢▢▢▢▢▢▢▢ . . .

(b) What is the position of the 18th orange square?

1 Without dividing, list the cloakroom ticket numbers which have as a factor
   (a) 5   (b) 4   (c) 6   (d) 8   (e) 9.

2 (a) Pierre arranges 12 identical tables with square tops in **3 rows of 4** to make a large rectangular table.

      In which other ways could Pierre have made a rectangular table?
   (b) List all the **factor pairs** for 12.

3 List all the factor pairs for
   (a) 18   (b) 20   (c) 30 (d) 36.

4 (a) What type of number is on each of these tickets?

        9   16   25   64   81   100

   (b) List all the factors for each number.
   (c) What do you notice about the number of factors for each number?

5 Find two numbers from 1 to 30 which have
   (a) only four factors   (b) only six factors   (c) only two factors.

1 Robert uses candles to make patterns of triangles.

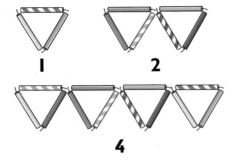

1   2   3

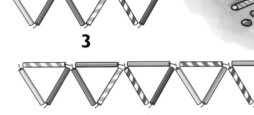

4   5

(a) Copy and complete this table:

Number of triangles	Number of candles
1 →	3
2 →	
3 →	
4 →	
5 →	

(b) How many candles are needed for
 ● 10 triangles   ● 100 triangles?

(c) Copy and complete this rule:

The number of candles is _____ times the number of triangles.

2 Robert also makes patterns of rhombuses.

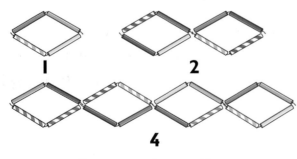

1   2   3

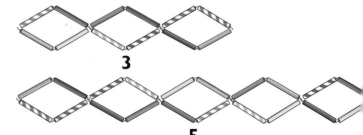

4   5

(a) Copy and complete this table:

Number of rhombuses	Number of candles
1 →	4
2 →	
3 →	
4 →	
5 →	

(b) How many candles are needed for
 ● 10 rhombuses   ● 50 rhombuses

(c) Copy and complete this rule:

The number of candles is _____ times the number of rhombuses.

(d) How many **rhombuses** can be made using
 ● 32 candles   ● 80 candles?

1 Robert makes these patterns of squares.

(a) Copy and complete this table:

(b) Write a rule for finding
- the number of candles when you know the number of squares
- the number of squares when you know the number of candles.

Number of squares	Number of candles
1 →	4
2 →	
3 →	
4 →	
5 →	
8 →	
11 →	

2 In these patterns Robert also uses chocolate drops.

  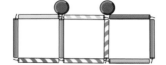 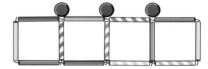

(a) Draw a table to show the **Number of squares** and the **Number of drops** when there are 1, 2, 3, 4, 6, 9 and 15 squares.

(b) Write a rule for finding
- the number of drops when you know the number of squares
- the number of squares when you know the number of drops.

(c) How many squares are there when there are • 19 drops • 99 drops?

3

(a) Draw a table to show the **Number of triangles** and the **Number of drops** when there are 1, 2, 3, 4, 7, 10 and 21 triangles.

(b) Write a rule for finding
- the number of drops when you know the number of triangles
- the number of triangles when you know the number of drops.

(c) How many triangles are there when there are • 52 drops • 101 drops?

Captain Nero
Lock-Keeper's Cottage
Canal Bank
Newkirk
NK66GY

1   Write True or False for each statement about
    the **number** from Captain Nero's postcode.

   (a)   The number is even.   (b)   It is a multiple of 5.
   (c)   It is a common multiple of 6 and 11.   (d)   One of its factors is 7.
   (e)   One of its factor pairs is 2 and 33.   (f)   It is a square number.

2   Match each person to the number from their postcode.

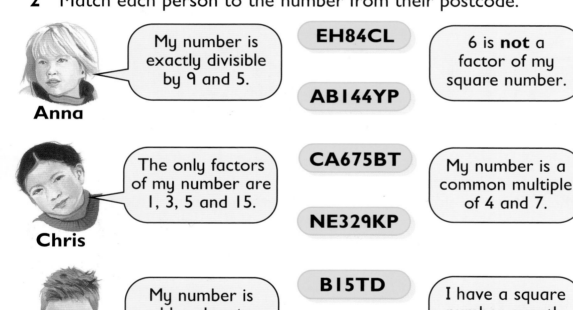

Anna — My number is exactly divisible by 9 and 5.

EH84CL

AB144YP

Bianca — 6 is **not** a factor of my square number.

Chris — The only factors of my number are 1, 3, 5 and 15.

CA675BT

NE329KP

Danny — My number is a common multiple of 4 and 7.

Ewan — My number is odd and **not** a multiple of 5.

B15TD

G64DB

Finlay — I have a square number exactly divisible by 9.

3   Describe the number from each of these postcodes in as many
    different ways as you can.

   (a) HX81CF   (b) PH45GZ   (c) LA216MA

1 Marston Bank first opened in the year 1750, when the town's population was 1000.
The population of Marston **doubled** every 25 years.

What was the population of Marston in the year 2000?

2 The total value of the tokens in the two bags is £2500.

How many tokens are **(a)** red   **(b)** blue?

3

The secret number which opens the safe door is
- greater than 675
- less than 725
- a multiple of 5
- divisible by 3 **and** by 9.

What is the secret number?

4 Ten local bankers attend a meeting at Marston Bank.

Each banker shakes hands with **all** of the others.
How many handshakes are there altogether?

5
- A security van visits Marston Bank every 6 days.
- A fax from Head Office arrives every 15 days.
- The secret number which opens the safe is changed every 10 days.

One week, **all three** of these things happen on the **same** day.
After how many more days will all three things happen on the same day again?

47

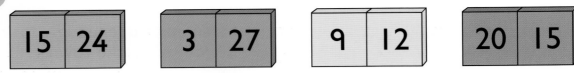

1 For which tile are **all** of these statements true?

- The product of the tile numbers is a three-digit number.
- The difference between the numbers is equal to one quarter of the larger number.
- Each number is a multiple of 3.

2 **(a)** Write a rule, involving multiplication and then subtraction, for using the numbers in the circles to make each number in the centre.

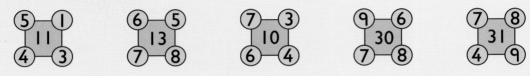

(b) Write a **different** rule for using the numbers in these circles to make each number in the centre.
Find the missing numbers.

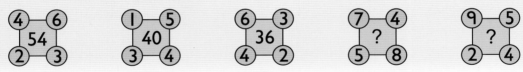

3 A magician has a box of tricks.
There are fewer than 100 tricks in his box.

When I count in fives there are no tricks left over.
When I count in sixes there is one trick left over.
When I count in sevens there is still one left over.

How many tricks are in the magician's box?

4

Which number from 1 to 10 can go through these three machines and be
(a) **the same** at the FINISH as it was at the START
(b) **twice as large** at the FINISH as it was at the START?

1 Write the equal fractions story for each pair of shapes.

(a)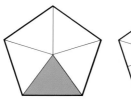

(b)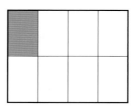

(c)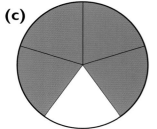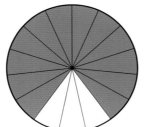

(d)

(e)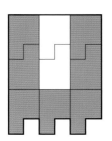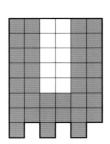

(f)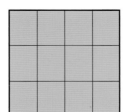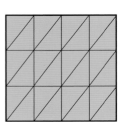

2 Copy and complete.

(a) $\dfrac{1}{2} = \dfrac{}{10}$

(b) $\dfrac{1}{5} = \dfrac{}{20}$

(c) $\dfrac{1}{10} = \dfrac{}{50}$

(d) $\dfrac{1}{7} = \dfrac{}{21}$

(e) $\dfrac{}{12} = \dfrac{3}{4}$

(f) $\dfrac{}{15} = \dfrac{2}{3}$

(g) $\dfrac{}{14} = \dfrac{2}{7}$

(h) $\dfrac{}{90} = \dfrac{4}{9}$

(i) $\dfrac{3}{6} = \dfrac{}{30}$

(j) $\dfrac{}{56} = \dfrac{6}{8}$

(k) $\dfrac{5}{10} = \dfrac{}{80}$

(l) $\dfrac{}{80} = \dfrac{3}{4}$

3 Change

(a) $\dfrac{1}{3}$ to sixths

(b) $\dfrac{1}{9}$ to eighteenths

(c) $\dfrac{7}{8}$ to eightieths

(d) $\dfrac{9}{10}$ to thirtieths

(e) $\dfrac{4}{6}$ to thirty-sixths

(f) $\dfrac{4}{10}$ to fortieths.

4 Write **three** other fractions equal to

(a) $\dfrac{1}{4}$

(b) $\dfrac{3}{5}$

(c) $\dfrac{4}{7}$

(d) $\dfrac{3}{3}$

1 Copy and complete.

(a) $\dfrac{3}{6} = \dfrac{}{2}$ (b) $\dfrac{2}{12} = \dfrac{}{6}$ (c) $\dfrac{6}{15} = \dfrac{}{5}$ (d) $\dfrac{8}{12} = \dfrac{}{3}$

(e) $\dfrac{}{7} = \dfrac{30}{35}$ (f) $\dfrac{}{9} = \dfrac{24}{27}$ (g) $\dfrac{}{4} = \dfrac{15}{20}$ (h) $\dfrac{}{10} = \dfrac{30}{50}$

(i) $\dfrac{24}{48} = \dfrac{}{8}$ (j) $\dfrac{}{4} = \dfrac{9}{36}$ (k) $\dfrac{40}{50} = \dfrac{}{5}$ (l) $\dfrac{}{9} = \dfrac{48}{72}$

2 Change

(a) $\dfrac{12}{18}$ to thirds   (b) $\dfrac{15}{40}$ to eighths   (c) $\dfrac{24}{32}$ to quarters

(d) $\dfrac{16}{20}$ to tenths   (e) $\dfrac{12}{36}$ to ninths   (f) $\dfrac{14}{49}$ to sevenths.

3 Which of these fractions are equal to   (a) $\dfrac{2}{3}$ (b) $\dfrac{3}{4}$ (c) $\dfrac{4}{5}$?

$\dfrac{24}{30}$ $\dfrac{60}{80}$ $\dfrac{20}{30}$ $\dfrac{33}{40}$ $\dfrac{20}{25}$ $\dfrac{21}{28}$ $\dfrac{36}{45}$ $\dfrac{25}{35}$ $\dfrac{16}{24}$

4 Simplify.

(a) $\dfrac{8}{16}$ (b) $\dfrac{6}{18}$ (c) $\dfrac{35}{50}$ (d) $\dfrac{15}{24}$ (e) $\dfrac{45}{81}$

(f) $\dfrac{30}{90}$ (g) $\dfrac{12}{84}$ (h) $\dfrac{28}{70}$ (i) $\dfrac{75}{90}$ (j) $\dfrac{84}{96}$

5 Ayub and Bea played 30 games of Noughts and Crosses. Ayub won 10 games, Bea won 6 games and the rest were draws.

What **fraction** of the games
(a) were won by Bea
(b) were won by Ayub
(c) were draws?

6 The table shows the results when Bea threw two dice 50 times.

What **fraction** of the throws resulted in
(a) an odd and an even number
(b) two odd numbers
(c) two even numbers?

Numbers on dice	Frequency
1 odd + 1 even	25
2 odd	10
2 even	15

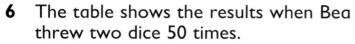

One tenth is smaller than one fifth.

One quarter is greater than one sixth.

1 Write > or < between each pair of fractions.

(a) $\frac{1}{3}$ and $\frac{1}{2}$ (b) $\frac{1}{6}$ and $\frac{1}{7}$ (c) $\frac{1}{12}$ and $\frac{1}{15}$ (d) $\frac{1}{20}$ and $\frac{1}{19}$

2 Write **three** fractions

(a) greater than one sixth   (b) smaller than one third.

3 Copy and complete.

(a) $\frac{1}{10}$ is ___ of $\frac{1}{5}$

$\frac{1}{5}$ is ___ $\frac{1}{10}$

(b) $\frac{1}{20}$ is ___ of $\frac{1}{10}$

$\frac{1}{10}$ is ___ $\frac{1}{20}$

$\frac{1}{6}$ is half of $\frac{1}{3}$

$\frac{1}{3}$ is twice $\frac{1}{6}$

(c) $\frac{1}{8}$ is ___ $\frac{1}{16}$

$\frac{1}{16}$ is ___ of $\frac{1}{8}$

(d) $\frac{1}{2}$ is ___ times $\frac{1}{6}$

$\frac{1}{6}$ is ___ of $\frac{1}{2}$

4 List the numbers in order.

(a) Start with the smallest.

$1\frac{1}{12}$ $2\frac{1}{3}$ $1\frac{2}{3}$ $2\frac{7}{12}$ $1\frac{1}{2}$

(b) Start with the largest.

$2\frac{3}{5}$ $3\frac{3}{10}$ $2\frac{9}{10}$ $2\frac{3}{4}$ $3\frac{1}{2}$

5 Copy this part of a number line which has 30 divisions.

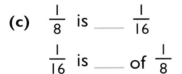

0

Label the positions of $\frac{1}{2}$ $\frac{3}{10}$ $\frac{2}{3}$ $\frac{1}{5}$ $\frac{9}{10}$ $\frac{1}{6}$ $\frac{11}{15}$

6 Write the number halfway between

(a) $\frac{3}{5}$ and $\frac{4}{5}$ (b) $\frac{1}{3}$ and $\frac{2}{3}$ (c) $3\frac{1}{4}$ and $3\frac{1}{2}$ (d) $4\frac{1}{2}$ and $4\frac{5}{8}$

7 Find a fraction

(a) greater than $\frac{1}{2}$ and less than $\frac{3}{5}$ (b) less than $\frac{1}{3}$ and greater than $\frac{1}{4}$

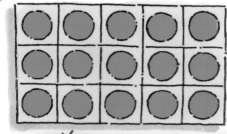

1 Find **(a)** $\frac{1}{3}$ of the circles   **(b)** $\frac{1}{5}$ of the circles

         (c) $\frac{1}{2}$ of the stars   **(d)** $\frac{1}{7}$ of the stars

         (e) $\frac{1}{4}$ of the triangles   **(f)** $\frac{1}{6}$ of the triangles.

2 **(a)** $\frac{3}{10}$ of 30   **(b)** $\frac{1}{8}$ of 48   **(c)** $\frac{1}{4}$ of 32   **(d)** one third of 18

    (e) $\frac{1}{9}$ of 63   **(f)** $\frac{1}{7}$ of 28   **(g)** $\frac{1}{6}$ of 54   **(h)** one fifth of 45

3 **(a)** $\frac{1}{6}$ of 420   **(b)** $\frac{1}{8}$ of 720   **(c)** $\frac{1}{7}$ of 490   **(d)** one ninth of 360

    (e) $\frac{1}{5}$ of 200   **(f)** $\frac{1}{4}$ of 360   **(g)** $\frac{1}{3}$ of 210   **(h)** one tenth of 900

4 Alison spent one eighth of her money on a packet of gold stars. How much money did she have?

1 Workers at *Peter's Petfoods* give $\frac{1}{100}$ of their bonus to the charity *Petcare*.
How much does each of these workers give to *Petcare*?

Bonus	Adam £400
Bonus	Baka £700
Bonus	Cara £1000
Bonus	Damon £1300

2 (a) $\frac{1}{100}$ of 300   (b) $\frac{1}{100}$ of 800   (c) $\frac{1}{100}$ of 100   (d) $\frac{1}{100}$ of 500

  (e) $\frac{1}{100}$ of 2000   (f) $\frac{1}{100}$ of 9000   (g) $\frac{1}{100}$ of 6000   (h) $\frac{1}{100}$ of 8600

  (i) $\frac{1}{100}$ of 3900   (j) $\frac{1}{100}$ of 6400   (k) $\frac{1}{100}$ of 4100   (l) $\frac{1}{100}$ of 5800

3 Write
- in centimetres

  (a) $\frac{52}{100}$ m   (b) $\frac{35}{100}$ m   (c) $\frac{90}{100}$ m

- in pence

  (a) £ $\frac{17}{100}$ (b) £ $\frac{24}{100}$ (c) £ $\frac{10}{100}$

4 What fraction is
  (a) 68 p of £1   (b) 99 p of £1   (c) 1 cm of 1 metre   (d) 50 cm of 1 metre?

5 Write (a) $\frac{1}{100}$ km in metres   (b) $\frac{1}{100}$ kg in grams   (c) $\frac{1}{100}$ ℓ in millilitres

6 How much was the **bonus** earned by each of these workers
at *Peter's Petfoods*?

I gave £5 to *Petcare*.

I gave £9.

I gave £12.

53

30 first class

36 second class

1 Find each fraction of the first class stamps.

(a) $\frac{1}{2}$ (b) $\frac{1}{5}$ (c) $\frac{2}{5}$ (d) $\frac{1}{6}$ (e) $\frac{5}{6}$ (f) $\frac{2}{3}$

2 Find each fraction of the second class stamps.

(a) $\frac{3}{4}$ (b) $\frac{1}{9}$ (c) $\frac{7}{9}$ (d) $\frac{1}{6}$ (e) $\frac{3}{6}$ (f) $\frac{2}{3}$

3 (a) $\frac{1}{100}$ of 600   (b) $\frac{3}{10}$ of 70   (c) $\frac{4}{5}$ of 45   (d) two thirds of 21

(e) $\frac{1}{7}$ of 56   (f) $\frac{3}{8}$ of 48   (g) $\frac{5}{6}$ of 42   (h) two ninths of 72

4 (a) $\frac{1}{4}$ of 80   (b) $\frac{3}{5}$ of 55   (c) $\frac{7}{10}$ of 300   (d) three quarters of 160

(e) $\frac{5}{8}$ of 800   (f) $\frac{2}{6}$ of 240   (g) $\frac{5}{9}$ of 450   (h) three sevenths of 280

5 Write

(a) $£\frac{2}{10}$ in pence   (b) $\frac{9}{10}$ km in metres   (c) $\frac{3}{10}$ kg in grams

(d) $\frac{17}{100}$ m in centimetres   (e) $\frac{9}{100}$ km in metres   (f) $\frac{5}{100}$ ℓ in millilitres.

6 (a) $\frac{4}{7}$ of 7m   (b) $\frac{9}{10}$ of 70 km   (c) $\frac{6}{8}$ of 32 ℓ (d) $\frac{3}{9}$ of 63 kg

(e) $\frac{1}{8}$ of £4   (f) $\frac{4}{5}$ of 2 m   (g) $\frac{8}{10}$ of 7 ℓ (h) $\frac{7}{8}$ of 2 kg

7 Write the value of each stamp as a fraction of £1.

8 What fraction is   (a) 70 cm of 1 m   (b) 45 cm of 1 m   (c) 140 cm of 1 m
(d) 200 m of 1 km   (e) 800 g of 1 kg   (f) 600 ml of 1 ℓ (g) 40 ml of 1 ℓ?

1 Write as a decimal fraction.

(a)  $\frac{3}{10}$

(b) $15\frac{7}{10}$

(c) $6\frac{9}{10}$

(d) $20\frac{1}{10}$

(e) three and six tenths

(f) seven and two tenths

(g) four tenths

(h) eighteen tenths

2 Copy and complete each sequence.

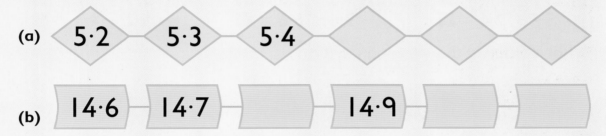

(a) 5·2 5·3 5·4

(b) 14·6 14·7 14·9

3 Write **a** number between:

(a) 3·4 and 3·7

(b) 10·2 and 9·7

(c) 4·4 and 4·8

(d) 11·1 and 10·8

4 Write in order. Start with the **smallest** number.

(a) 2·3 3·2 1·3 3·3

(b) 46·5 65·4 56·4 45·6 54·6

5 Write in order. Start with the **largest** number.

(a) 29·7 72·9 97·2 27·9

(b) 42·6 64·2 26·4 62·4 46·2

6

16.7   8.4   4.8   26.5

25.0   33.4   54.6   19.3

Which number has

(a) 3 tenths

(b) 5 units

(c) 3 tens

(d) the largest tenths digit

(e) a tenths digit half of the units digit?

Ask your teacher for the rules to the games.

Decimal Bingo

8·5	5·8	9·3
5·5	8·1	7·3

7·3	9·0	4·2
9·5	5·8	7·6

9·3	5·0	5·8
8·5	8·0	9·5

1
(a) $4·2 + 1·6 = \blacksquare$
(b) $1·4 + 2·8 = \blacksquare$
(c) $2·7 + 2·8 = \blacksquare$
(d) $6·3 + 1·7 = \blacksquare$
(e) $1·7 + 5·6 = \blacksquare$
(f) $2·9 + 6·4 = \blacksquare$
(g) $3·2 + 4·4 = \blacksquare$
(h) $1·2 + 3·8 = \blacksquare$
(i) $7·1 + 2·4 = \blacksquare$
(j) $5·7 + 2·4 = \blacksquare$
(k) $3·4 + 5·6 = \blacksquare$
(l) $4·2 + 4·3 = \blacksquare$

2 What colour is the winning card?

Noughts and Crosses

1·6	4·8	1·7
4·4	5·0	3·0
3·3	2·6	2·1

3 Xena plays first. Who wins the game?

Xena
(a) $7·5 - 2·5 = \blacksquare$
(c) $5·8 - 1·4 = \blacksquare$
(e) $3·2 - 1·5 = \blacksquare$
(g) $5·0 - 2·4 = \blacksquare$
(i) $8·4 - 3·6 = \blacksquare$

Oliver
(b) $6·3 - 4·2 = \blacksquare$
(d) $9·8 - 6·8 = \blacksquare$
(f) $7·2 - 3·9 = \blacksquare$
(h) $6·1 - 4·5 = \blacksquare$
(j) $9·0 - 4·7 = \blacksquare$

Rows and Columns

4 Copy and complete so that each row **and** column has a total of 10.

(a)

3·2		4·0
	6·3	1·6
4·7		

(b)

	3·3	
4·7		4·3
	5·7	

Name each winner of Games I to 4.

Game I The player with the highest score wins.

84·2 + 13·6
Sally

57·5 + 42·4
John

73·1 + 24·6
Mary

64·2 + 35·6
Harry

Game 2 The player with lowest score wins.

64·7 – 13·1
Jan

86·4 – 35·2
Brad

78·7 – 22·6
Lisa

98·5 – 44·3
Leo

Game 3 The player with the highest score wins.

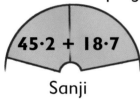 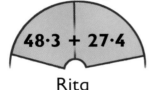  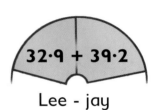

45·2 + 18·7
Sanji

48·3 + 27·4
Rita

26·8 + 37·5
Paulo

32·9 + 39·2
Lee - jay

Game 4 The player with the lowest score wins.

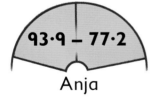 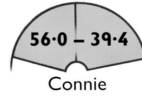 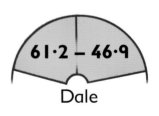

93·9 – 77·2
Anja

38·1 – 13·9
Barry

56·0 – 39·4
Connie

61·2 – 46·9
Dale

Give the colour of the winning cards in Games 5 and 6.

Game 5 The value of the winning cards is less than 26·9.

8·6 + 18·7

53·4 – 26·5

14·9 + 13·3

80·4 – 53·8

Game 6 The value of the winning card is greater than 82.

42·3 + 35·8

101 – 25·7

91·6 – 9·8

37·4 + 46·9

foodpack 1·2 kg

ice-axe 2·3 kg

fuel can 6·8 kg

rope 5·4 kg

water bottle 3·7 kg

1 Find the weight of

(a) 4 food packs	**(b)** 3 ice-axes	**(c)** 2 ropes
(d) 5 fuel cans	**(e)** 6 food packs	**(f)** 7 water bottles
(g) 8 ice-axes	**(h)** 9 ropes	**(i)** 3 fuel cans.

2

(a) $2 \times 3·7 = \blacksquare$	**(b)** $4 \times 3·4 = \blacksquare$	**(c)** $7 \times 2·5 = \blacksquare$	**(d)** $8 \times 1·9 = \blacksquare$
(e) $4·3 \times 5 = \blacksquare$	**(f)** $2·8 \times 9 = \blacksquare$	**(g)** $9·1 \times 3 = \blacksquare$	**(h)** $3·4 \times 6 = \blacksquare$
(i) $3 \times \blacksquare = 4·8$	**(j)** $6 \times \blacksquare = 8·4$	**(k)** $1·1 \times \blacksquare = 7·7$	**(l)** $2·4 \times \blacksquare = 9·$

3

(a) Double 2·3	**(b)** Twice 1·9	**(c)** Double 4·6	**(d)** Twice 8·4
(e) $\blacksquare \times 2 = 3·6$	**(f)** $\blacksquare \times 2 = 5·2$	**(g)** $2 \times \blacksquare = 10·8$	**(h)** $2 \times \blacksquare = 15$

4 On **Wednesday**

- Team A walked twice as far as they did on Monday
- Team B doubled the distance they walked on Tuesday.

How far did each team walk during the three days?.

	Distance walked on	
	Monday	Tuesday
Team A	4·6 km	7·1 km
Team B	8·5 km	3·4 km

1 How many litres altogether are in

(a) 3 cans of petrol
(b) 2 drums of engine oil
(c) 4 bottles of anti-freeze
(d) 7 tins of brake fluid
(e) 5 drums of engine oil
(f) 8 cans of petrol
(g) 9 tins of brake fluid
(h) 6 bottles of anti-freeze?

2 **(a)** 17·3 × 5 **(b)** 2 × 45·1 **(c)** 13·6 × 7 **(d)** 4 × 21·6
(e) 6 × 14·9 **(f)** 10·4 × 9 **(g)** 3 × 26·3 **(h)** 11·9 × 8

3 The jet-wash uses 12·3 litres of water for each wash.
How much water is used for

(a) 5 washes **(b)** 8 washes?

4 A shelf can safely hold up to 215 kg in weight.
Is it safe for the shelf to hold 6 tyres each weighing 34·7 kg?
Explain.

1   Alex shares the food equally among 10 boxes.
    Find the weight of food in each box.

(a)    (b)    (c)

2   (a) $24 \div 10 = \blacksquare$ (b) $8 \div 10 = \blacksquare$ (c) $63 \div 10 = \blacksquare$ (d) $31 \div 10 = \blacksquare$
    (e) $\blacksquare \div 10 = 0.2$ (f) $\blacksquare \div 10 = 4.5$ (g) $\blacksquare \div 10 = 6.9$ (h) $\blacksquare \div 10 = 7.1$

3   (a) $\frac{1}{2}$ of 4.8 (b) half of 5.4 (c) $\frac{1}{2}$ of 7

    (d) $\blacksquare \div 2 = 1.5$ (e) $\blacksquare \div 2 = 3.9$ (f) $\blacksquare \div 2 = 4.6$

4   (a) 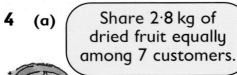 Share 2·8 kg of dried fruit equally among 7 customers.

    (b) Share 7·2 ℓ of olive oil equally among 9 customers.

 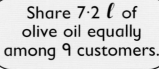  

5   (a) $2.4 \div 3$ (b) $1.8 \div 2$ (c) $4.5 \div 5$ (d) $7.2 \div 8$
    (e) $4.2 \div 7$ (f) $3.6 \div 6$ (g) $6.3 \div 9$ (h) $3.2 \div 4$

6   (a) $1.8 \div 3 = \blacksquare$ (b) $4.2 \div 6 = \blacksquare$ (c) $6.4 \div 8 = \blacksquare$ (d) $3.6 \div 4 = \blacksquare$
    (e) $3.5 \div \blacksquare = 0.7$ (f) $5.4 \div \blacksquare = 0.6$ (g) $2.8 \div \blacksquare = 0.7$ (h) $5.6 \div \blacksquare = 0.8$

Bi-tec Laboratories

1 These chemicals are shared equally among Bi-tec's scientists.

| 13·8 kg Obron | 48·5 kg Valspa | 23·7 kg Revus | 30·1 kg Lithion | 22·8 kg Zortz |

Find how many kilograms each scientist receives.

(a) Obron between 2 scientists (b) Valspa among 5 scientists
(c) Revus among 3 scientists (d) Lithion among 7 scientists
(e) Zortz among 6 scientists.

2 Share the Vizone equally. What volume does each lab receive?

(a) 44·7ℓ of red Vizone among 3 labs
(b) 92ℓ of blue Vizone among 8 labs
(c) 96·3ℓ of yellow Vizone among 9 labs
(d) 74ℓ of green Vizone among 4 labs

3 (a) $14·7 \div 3$ (b) $93 \div 2$ (c) $34 \div 4$ (d) $55·2 \div 6$
(e) $94·4 \div 8$ (f) $76·3 \div 7$ (g) $77·5 \div 5$ (h) $48·6 \div 9$

4 A scientist has made some mistakes. Find each error and correct it.

(a) $\dfrac{52·8 \text{ kg}}{6} = 8·7 \text{ kg}$ (b) $\dfrac{81·9 \text{ kg}}{7} = 10·7 \text{ kg}$ (c) $\dfrac{91 \text{ kg}}{5} = 18·2 \text{ kg}$

(d) $\dfrac{28·8\,\ell}{9} = 3·2\ell$ (e) $\dfrac{89·6\,\ell}{8} = 11·3\ell$ (f) $\dfrac{99·6\,\ell}{4} = 24·8\ell$

1 List the first eight numbers in each sequence.

(a) Start at 0. Count on 0·1 each time.

(b)  Start at 2. Count on 0·5 each time.

(c) 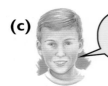 Start at 4. Count 0·25 each time.

(d)  Start at 10. Count **back** 0·1 each time.

(e)  Start at 8. Count back 0·5 each time.

(f) Start at 6. Count back 0·25 each time.

2 Copy and complete each sequence.
- (a) 0·92, 0·94, 0·96, ■, ■, ■, 1·04
- (b) 1·76, 1·77, 1·78, ■, ■, ■, 1·82
- (c) 2·54, 2·52, 2·50, ■, ■, ■, 2·42
- (d) 3·04, 3·03, 3·02, ■, ■, ■, 2·98

3 Write the 2-place decimal fraction
- (a) before 6·48
- (b) after 7·35
- (c) before 5·86
- (d) after 3·24
- (e) before 8·21
- (f) after 1·69.

4 Write the 2-place decimal fraction between
- (a) 0·47 and 0·49
- (b) 3·58 and 3·60
- (c) 5·99 and 6·01.

5 Write **a** 2-place decimal fraction between
- (a) 0·67 and 0·74
- (b) 1·81 and 1·9
- (c) 3·9 and 4·05.

6 Write each decimal as a mixed number.

(a) 2 4•7

(b) 2•4 1

(c) 5•8 9

(d) 7 8•3

(e) 5 0•2

(f) 3•6 3

(g) 4 7•5

(h) 6•0 5

$16·3 = 16\frac{3}{10}$

$4·58 = $

30·6   45·8   3·24   6·38   1·75

4·52   13·9

I Which number has

(a) 2 tenths   (b) 5 hundredths
(c) 7 units   (d) 4 tens
(e) the largest tenths digit
(f) the smallest tenths digit
(g) a units digit double the tenths digit
(h) a hundredths digit half of the tenths digit?

0·46   8·07

97·4   2·63

2 Write the value of each red digit.

(a) 7·16   (b) 16·7   (c) 1·67

(d) 43·8   (e) 6·92   (f) 5·05

3 Which is the largest number?

(a) 2·48 2·84 2·80   (b) 6·76 6·7 6·75   (c) 2·31 3·12 3·21

4 Which is the smallest number?

(a) 6·51 6·15 6·5   (b) 8·75 8·7 8·57   (c) 4·3 4·35 4·53

5 Write the numbers in order.

• Start with the smallest.

(a) 0·58, 0·40, 0·53, 0·61, 0·42   (b) 0·2, 0·06, 0·14, 0·09, 0·1
(c) 5·99, 6·43, 4·63, 4·36, 6·34, 6·06 (d) 9·9, 9·01, 0·19, 9·1, 0·91, 9·09

• Start with the largest.

(e) 0·73, 0·62, 0·8, 0·7, 0·75   (f) 0·9, 1·05, 0·98, 1·08, 1·0
(g) 7·59, 9·75, 7·79, 9·95, 9·57, 7·95 (h) 8·8, 8·02, 0·28, 8·2, 0·82, 8·08

Tiddlywinks Championships

0.52m   0.45m   0.64m   0.6m
0.35m   0.41m   0.5m
0.68m   0.83m
0.31m   0.46m
0.7m

1 **(a)** Find the total distance, in metres, each player's counter has jumped.
(b) The cup is 2 metres from each player. How far, in metres, does each player's counter still have to jump to reach it?

2 Find the missing numbers.

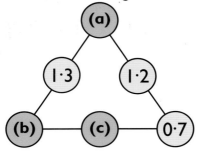

Each side of the triangle has a total of 3.

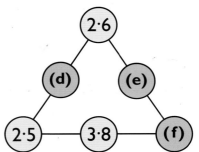

Each side of the triangle has a total of 8.

3 Find the sum of the numbers on each counter.

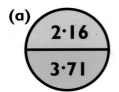 (a) 2·16 / 3·71

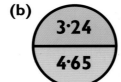 (b) 3·24 / 4·65

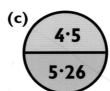 (c) 4·5 / 5·26

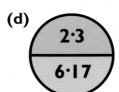 (d) 2·3 / 6·17

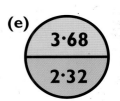 (e) 3·68 / 2·32

4 **(a)** $5·62 + \blacksquare = 6$ **(b)** $\blacksquare + 7·18 = 8$ **(c)** $6·52 + \blacksquare = 6·6$
(d) $2·14 + \blacksquare = 2·2$ **(e)** $\blacksquare + 1·32 = 4·75$ **(f)** $2·47 + \blacksquare = 4·87$

5 Write **three** different addition stories using these numbers.

(a) Use 2 numbers each time.
(b) Use 4 numbers each time.

| 1·06 | 2·7 | 0·4 | 6·48 | 32·3 |

Sponsored games - money raised

Class 6

	Snakes & Ladders	Ludo	Connect 4	Beetle Drive	Tiddly-winks
Red team	£6·32	£5·51	£3·47	£21·50	£12·46
Blue team	£3·85	£7·07	£6·13	£23·35	£11·62
Yellow team	£3·62	£8·85	£5·31	£13·72	£12·02
Green team	£4·40	£4·32	£3·52	£14·33	£13·67

1 How much money did each team raise playing

(a) *Snakes and Ladders* and *Connect 4*
(b) *Ludo* and *Tiddlywinks*
(c) *Beetle Drive* and *Tiddlywinks*?

2 How much money altogether was raised
- by the red and blue teams playing
  (a) *Snakes and Ladders*　(b) *Tiddlywinks*
- by the yellow and green teams playing
  (c) *Snakes and Ladders*　(d) *Beetle Drive*　(e) *Ludo*?

3 Which team did each of these children play for?

(a)
My team raised £40·24 altogether.

(b)
My team raised the most money.

(c)
My team raised between £49 and £50.

(d)
My team raised £3·52 more than £40.

Work with a partner.
Game 1

0·75	0·42	0·3	0·89
0·9	Find the difference between a **blue** number and a **green** number.		0·13
0·56			0·98
0·21	0·67	0·34	0·8

Game 2

6·97	2·51	1·42	4·85
9·59	Subtract a **red** number from a **orange** number.		3·35
4·04			7·68
2·24	8·76	3·13	6·7

Game 3

0·65	2·76	0·25	0·92
1·45	Find pairs of numbers with a difference of 0·4.		3·56
3·16			1·05
1·32	4·36	3·96	0·52

Health Club Prices

	Swimming Pool	Multi-gym	Running Track	Raquet Sports	Ball Games
Day ticket	£6·84	£7·38	£4·52	£3·26	£2·85
Weekly ticket	£28·32	£33·89	£20·95	£11·40	£12·76
Monthly ticket	£83·28	£95·56	£73·80	£42·34	£48·04

1 Find the difference in price between
- day tickets for

    (a) the Swimming Pool and the Running Track
    (b) the Multi-gym and Raquet Sports

- weekly tickets for

    (c) Ball Games and the Multi-gym
    (d) the Running Track and Raquet Sports

- monthly tickets for

    (e) the Swimming Pool and the Multi-gym
    (f) the Running Track and Ball Games.

2 For each activity find the difference between the prices of

    (a) a weekly ticket and a day ticket
    (b) a monthly ticket and a weekly ticket.

3 How much does each person have left?

(a)

I had £50. I bought a weekly ticket for the Multi-gym.

(b)

I had £100. I bought a monthly ticket for Raquet Sports.

Garden Warehouse

Bug Scram 1·6 ℓ   Weed Zap 0·9 ℓ   Bloom Blast 1·25 ℓ   Leaf Shine 0·83 ℓ

1 What is the total volume of liquid in:

(a) 10

(b) 10

(c) 10

(d) 10

(e) 100   (f) 100   (g) 100   (h) 100   ?

2
(a) $10 \times 3·7$
(b) $10 \times 6·2$
(c) $18·4 \times 10$
(d) $6·41 \times 10$

(e) $100 \times 5·9$
(f) $100 \times 78·1$
(g) $0·42 \times 100$
(h) $4·06 \times 100$

(i) $\blacksquare \times 2·8 = 28$
(j) $0·16 \times \blacksquare = 16$
(k) $\blacksquare \times 10 = 53$
(l) $100 \times \blacksquare = 108$

3

Pansies 6·4 g   Lobelia 3·7 g   Sweet Peas 8·1 g   Marigolds 5·9 g   Cornflowers 7·2 g

Find the weight of seeds in

(a) 20 packets of   • Pansies   • Lobelia   • Marigolds

(b) 30 packets of   • Sweet Peas   • Marigolds   • Cornflowers

(c) 70 packets of   • Pansies   • Sweet Peas   • Marigolds

(d) 90 packets of   • Lobelia   • Sweet Peas   • Cornflowers.

4
(a) $3·2 \times 40$
(b) $1·7 \times 50$
(c) $80 \times 6·3$
(d) $60 \times 7·4$

(e) $0·51 \times 70$
(f) $0·68 \times 20$
(g) $30 \times 0·49$
(h) $50 \times 0·35$

(i) $0·06 \times 90$
(j) $80 \times 8·6$
(k) $40 \times 10·3$
(l) $70 \times 10·2$

5 Find the total cost of 30 tomato plants and 20 strawberry plants.

£1·40   Tomato   Strawberry   £0·65

S H O P   A T
www.**things.co.**

68

£12·35   £9·80   £28·65

£69   £33·40   £6·70

1 You have £100 to spend at www.*things.co.*
Make up an order where you spend as close to £100 as possible.
You cannot overspend.

2 What is the total cost of

   (a) 18 padlocks   **(b)** 13 calculators   **(c)** 11 watches?

3 Jack saved the same amount of money each month for one year.
How much did he save each month to buy the mobile phone?

4 Zara has saved £19·27 to buy the watch.
How much more does she need to save?

5 The cost of posting
one CD is £3·35.
What is the cost of posting
a CD to 27 customers?

6 What is the cost of two mobile phones in the Special Offer?

www.things.co.   www.things.co.   www.things.co.   www.things.co.

Special Offer!

Order two mobile phones and save $\frac{1}{4}$ of the cost.

Each pet blanket sold at
Petcare has **100 equal parts**.

1   Find the percentage of each
of these blankets

• coloured   • not coloured.

(a)   **(b)**

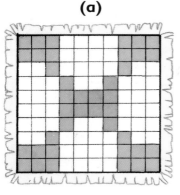   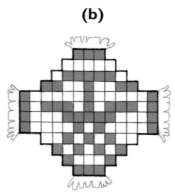

(c)

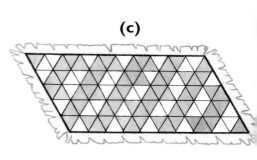

2   Find the percentage of each blanket
• coloured yellow   • coloured blue   • coloured   • not coloured.

(a)   **(b)**   **(c)**

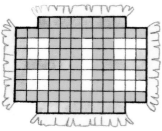   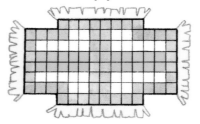   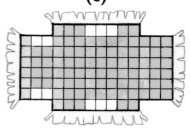

3   What percentage of
this blanket is

(a)   coloured
(b)   not coloured
(c)   neither blue nor geen
(d)   neither yellow nor blue
(e)   neither green nor yellow?

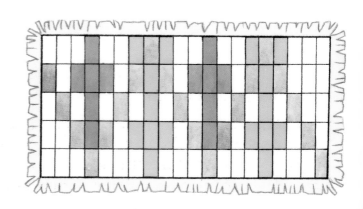

1 Write as a percentage.

(a) $\frac{17}{100}$ (b) $\frac{53}{100}$ (c) $\frac{6}{100}$ (d) $\frac{60}{100}$

(e) 0·26 (f) 0·95 (g) 0·70 (h) 0·07

2 Write in **two** other ways.

(a) 16% (b) $\frac{8}{100}$ (c) 0·4 (d) 0·01

(e) $\frac{23}{100}$ (f) 5% (g) 10% (h) 1

3 Write the percentage of each cat food which is **not** fish.

(a) PURR 14% fish

(b) Kat-Kit 26% fish

(c) Moggy 32% fish

4

Petcare

Customer Information

35% own a dog.
48% own a cat.
None owns both.

7% of dog owners have a Labrador.

63% of tropical fish owners have Angel Fish.

59% of cat owners have one cat and 22% have 2 cats.

What percentage of

(a) tropical fish owners do not have Angel Fish
(b) dog owners have breeds other than Labrador
(c) cat owners have three or more cats
(d) customers own neither a dog nor a cat?

1 For each shape, write the amount coloured
as a fraction **and** as a percentage.

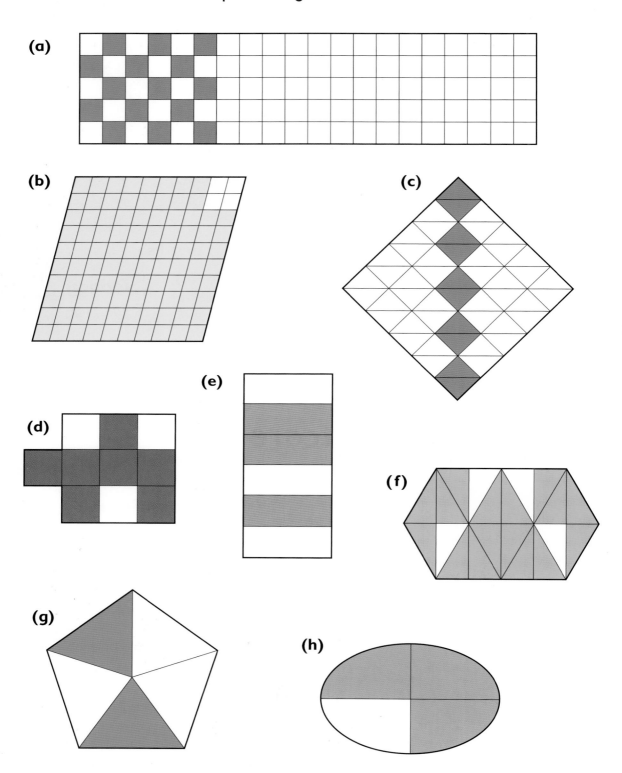

(a)

(b)

(c)

(e)

(d)

(f)

(g)

(h)

1 Write as a fraction **and** as a percentage
   (a) 10 out of 100   (b) 1 out of 100   (c) 35 out of 100
   (d) 10 out of 20   (e) 10 out of 40   (f) 6 out of 30
   (g) 30 out of 40   (h) 40 out of 80   (i) 50 out of 200.

2 Find
   (a) 10% of 50   (b) 10% of 20   (c) 10% of 100
   (d) 20% of 80   (e) 30% of 60   (f) 40% of 200
   (g) 70% of 30   (h) 90% of 70   (i) 60% of 500.

3 Find the weight in each bag of • protein • fat.

Cat Crunch
50% protein
25% fat

(a) Cat Crunch 300g
(b) Cat Crunch 480g
(c) Cat Crunch 600g

4 Which tin contains the greatest weight **of meat**?

ROVER 70% meat 400g
WOOF 75% meat 340g
BOW-WOW 60% meat 450g

5

Petcake birdcake
• Forty-five hundredths lard
• Three tenths seeds and nuts
• One quarter raisins

What **percentage** of birdcake is
(a) **not** lard   (b) **not** seeds and nuts   (c) **not** raisins?

1 Write each time as a 24 – hour time.

(a) 1.15pm

(b) 10.31am

(c) 11.05pm

(d) 9.07pm

(e) 7.51am

(f) 12 noon

2 Write each time as a 12 – hour time. Use **am** or **pm**.

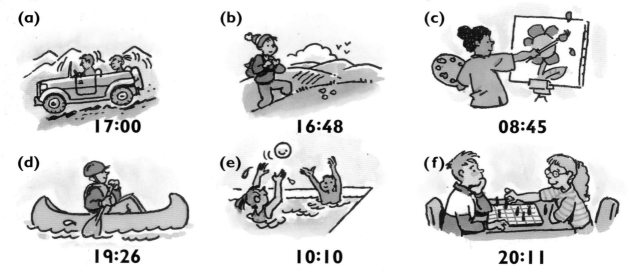

(a) 17:00

(b) 16:48

(c) 08:45

(d) 19:26

(e) 10:10

(f) 20:11

3 Find the missing times.

12 - hour time	6.18 pm	(b)	(c)	12.05 am
24 - hour time	(a)	09:43	14:56	(d)

4 Write these times in order. Start with the earliest.

4.23 pm   10:16   12.01 am   20:38   10.16 pm   04:19

1 Use the events on the notice board to make a programme for tomorrow.
Write all the times as **24-hour** times.

2 Which event takes place

(a) 1st　　　(b) 4th　　　(c) 7th　　　(d) last?

3 Which event starts

(a) 30 minutes after 11.02am　　(b) 15 minutes before 16:08
(c) 20 minutes after 8.43am　　(d) 25 minutes before 00:18?

4 Which events take place between

(a) 15:00 and 17:00　　(b) 07:00 and 09:00
(c) 11:15 and 15:15　　(d) 11:29 and 13:29?

1 Write the time

(a) 25 min after

(b) 40 min after

(c) 65 min after

(d) 80 min after

(e) 1h and 15 min after

(f) 1h and 50 min after

(g) 35 min before

(h) 50 min before

(i) 75 min before

(j) 90 min before

(k) 1h and 20 min before

(l) 1h and 45 min before

2 How many minutes are there between each **Start** and **Finish** time?

(a) Start → Finish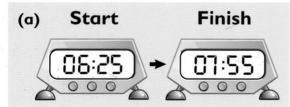

(b) Start → Finish

(c)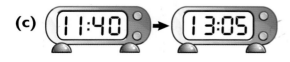

(d)

(e)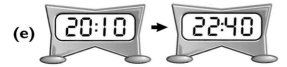

(f)

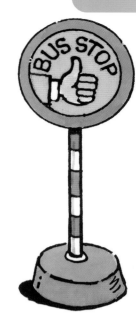

Bus Station	08:05	08:55	11:15	14:30
City Centre	08:20	09:20	11:25	14:40
Eldon	08:40	09:45	11:40	15:55
Lanbow	09:20	10:20	12:15	16:25
Walston	09:50	10:45	12:35	16:50
Ashford	10:15	11:10	12:55	17:15

1 How long does it take

(a) the 08:05 bus to reach the City Centre

(b) the 08:55 bus to reach Eldon

(c) the 11:15 bus to reach Walston?

2 How long is the journey time between

(a) Lanbow and Ashford on the 11:15 bus

(b) City Centre and Walston on the 14:30 bus?

3 The 11:15 bus is 20 minutes late leaving Eldon.
At what time does it arrive in Ashford?

4 Lisa boards the 08:05 bus at City Centre.
She gets off 90 minutes later.
Where does she get off the bus?

5 Sunil got off the bus at Ashford at 11:10.
His journey had taken 110 minutes.
Where did he board the bus? City center

6 An overnight 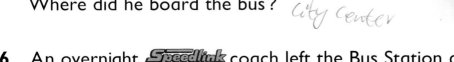 coach left the Bus Station at 19:30.
It arrived in Croxford at 06:30.
How long did the journey take?

I For how many seconds has each person been exercising?

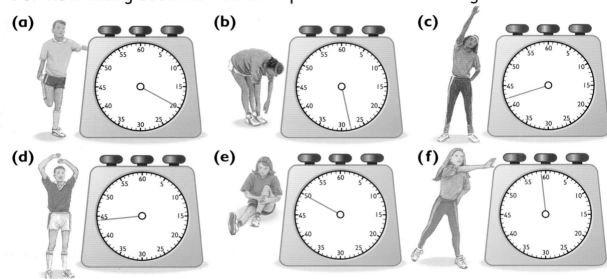

(a)   (b)   (c)

(d)   (e)   (f)

2 Elsa has been running for **18 minutes and 34 seconds.**

How long has Elsa spent on each activity?

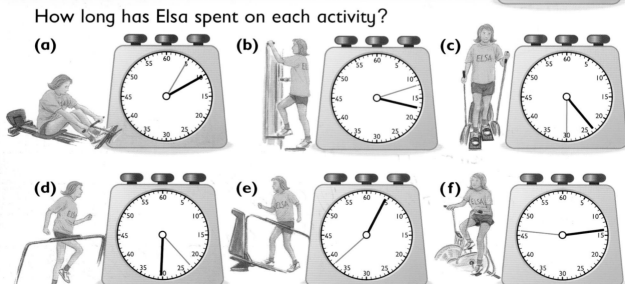

(a)   (b)   (c)

(d)   (e)   (f)

Work in pairs.

I   Use a stopclock or a
    watch which measures
    time in seconds.

(a)   You have **15 seconds** for each activity.
      How many times can you

- write this set of letters
  a e i o u

- toss and catch a coin

(b)   You have **30 seconds** for each activity.
      How many

- pegs can you put on
  a pegboard

- numbers can you list in order,
  starting at 100?
  100, 101, 102, 103, ...

(c)   You have **1 minute** for each activity.
      How many

- stick people can you
  draw

- times can you write this
  word?
  challenge

2   Copy the table.

(a)   Estimate then measure,
      in seconds, the time
      you take to complete
      each activity.

(b)   Complete the table
      for your results.

Activity	Time taken	
	Estimate	Measure
20 toe-touches		
50 skips		
30 bench-steps		
40 hops		

The yellow brick is $2\frac{1}{2}$ centimetres long.

1 What is the length of the yellow brick in **millimetres**?

2 Measure each length. Write it in centimetres **and** in millimetres.

(a)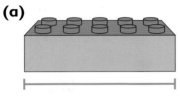

(b)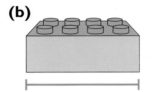

(c)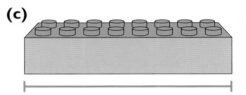

(d)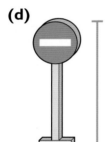

(e)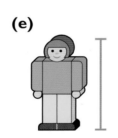

(f)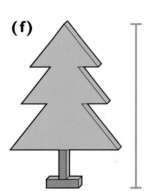

3 Write in millimetres.

(a) 7cm   (b) $10\frac{1}{2}$ cm   (c) 15cm   (d) $16\frac{1}{2}$ cm   (e) $20\frac{1}{2}$ cm

4 Write in centimetres.

(a) 90mm   (b) 65mm   (c) 120mm   (d) 145mm   (e) 305mm

5 Find the distance between the arrows in cm **and** in mm.

(a)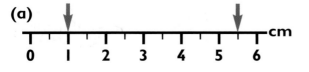

(b)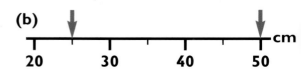

1 Measure and record each caterpillar's length
  • in millimetres only   • in centimetres and millimetres.

(a)    (b)    (c)

(d) 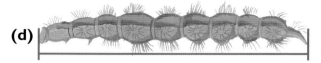   (e)

2 Write in millimetres.
  (a) 3 cm 7 mm   (b) 15 cm 9 mm   (c) 8 cm 1 mm   (d) 10 cm 4 mm

3 Write in centimetres and millimetres.
  (a) 58 mm   (b) 16 mm   (c) 153 mm   (d) 205 mm

4 The wingspan of the butterfly is
32 mm or 3 cm 2 mm or 3·2 cm.

Measure each wingspan in millimetres.
Write each measurement in **three** ways.

(a)    (b)    (c)

5 Draw caterpillars with lengths of
  (a) 26 mm   (b) 4·3 cm   (c) 7·4 cm   (d) 58 mm

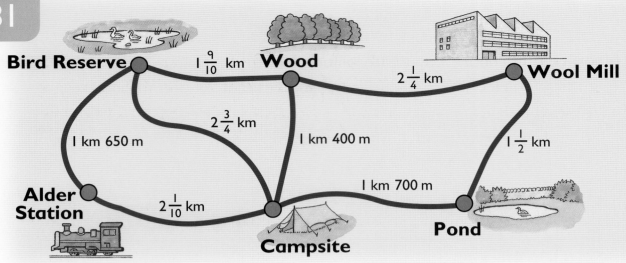

1 Write **in metres** the shortest distance between

   (a) the Wood and the Pond   **(b)** the Mill and the Campsite

   (c) the Station and the Wood   **(d)** the Bird Reserve and the Pond.

2 Find the total distance, in metres, of each of these journeys.

   (a) Station ⟶ Bird Reserve ⟶ Wood ⟶ Mill

   (b) Wood ⟶ Mill ⟶ Pond ⟶ Campsite

   (c) Mill ⟶ Wood ⟶ Campsite ⟶ Bird Reserve

3 The distance from Alder to Linton is 6 km 300 m.

Write the distance, in
kilometres and metres, from

   (a) Bagley to Entworth

   (b) Bagley to Linton

   (c) Alder to Bagley

   (d) Linton to Entworth.

	Linton	Entworth	Bagley
Alder	6300 m	7423 m	4008 m
Bagley	9040 m	4180 m	
Entworth	5706 m		

4 **(a)** Which two reels of wool have
a total length of $7\frac{1}{2}$ km?

   (b) Which three reels have a total
length of 11 km?

1 Which of these units of length would be best to use for each measurement?

millimetres	centimetres	metres	kilometres

(a)

length of your shoe

(b)

length of a lorry

(c)

distance around
your head

(d)

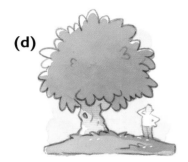

height of a tree

(e)

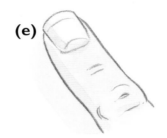

length of your
fingernail

(f)

distance between Paris
and London

2 Write another item you would measure in

   (a) metres   **(b)** millimetres   **(c)** kilometres   **(d)** centimetres.

3  Each book is 17 mm thick.
Would a set of 30 of these books
fit on a shelf 50 cm long?
Explain.

4 Mary walked 2 kilometres.
David walked 300 m less than Mary.
Tina walked 750 m more than David.
Find the distance walked by **(a)** David **(b)** Tina.

5 Ben's rope is 4 metres longer than Sue's.
Their ropes have a total length of 20 m.

How long is **(a)** Ben's rope **(b)** Sue's rope?

1 **Measure** to find each perimeter. Write it
- in millimetres only
- in centimetres only.

(a)

(b)
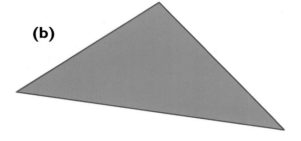

(c)
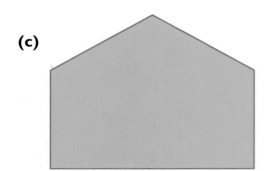

(d)

2 **Calculate** the perimeter of each shape.

(a)
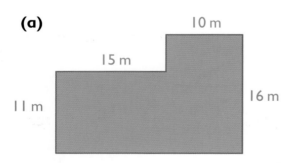

(b)
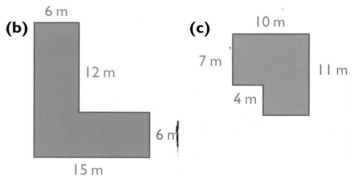

(c)
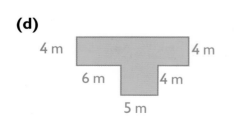

(d)
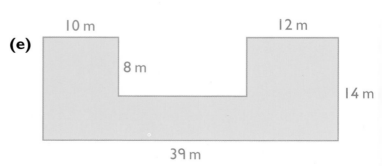

(e)

1 **Calculate** the perimeter of each shape.

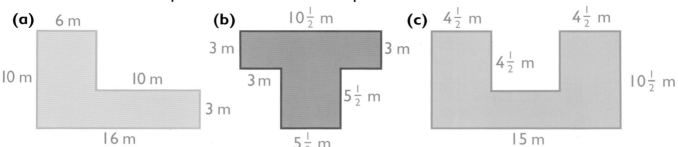

(a) 6 m, 10 m, 10 m, 16 m, 3 m

(b) $10\frac{1}{2}$ m, 3 m, 3 m, 3 m, 3m, $5\frac{1}{2}$ m, $5\frac{1}{2}$ m

(c) $4\frac{1}{2}$ m, $4\frac{1}{2}$ m, $4\frac{1}{2}$ m, $10\frac{1}{2}$ m, 15 m

2 **(a)** **Measure** the length and breadth of each rectangle in centimetres. Copy and complete the table

Rectangle	Length	Breadth	Perimeter
A			
B			
C			

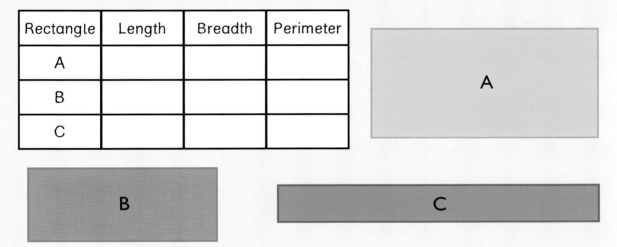

(b) How can you calculate the perimeter of a rectangle when you know its length and breadth?

3 **(a)** Measure the perimeter of each **regular** polygon in centimetres.

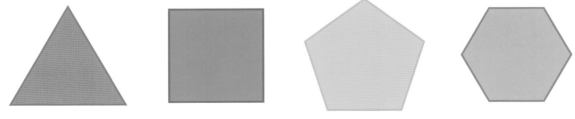

(b) How can you find the perimeter of a **regular** polygon?

4 **Calculate** the side length of this regular octagon.

Perimeter 80 cm

1 Write the weight of each item in kilograms, to the nearest $\frac{1}{10}$ kg **and** in grams, to the nearest 100 g.

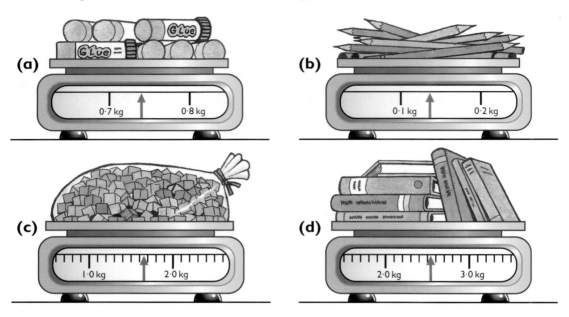

(a)   0·7 kg   0·8 kg

(b)   0·1 kg   0·2 kg

(c)   1·0 kg   2·0 kg

(d)   2·0 kg   3·0 kg

2 Write each weight in grams, to the nearest 100 g **and** in kilograms, to the nearest $\frac{1}{10}$ kg.

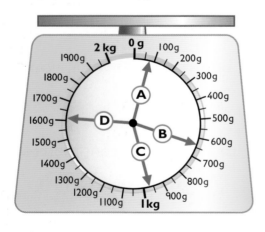

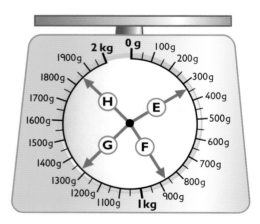

3 Find the weight of some containers
  • in grams, to the nearest 100 g
  • in kilograms, to the nearest $\frac{1}{10}$ kg.

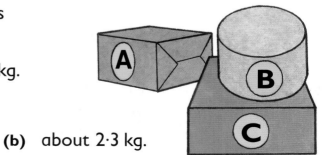

4 Find an object that weighs
  (a) between 0·8 kg and 1·0 kg   **(b)** about 2·3 kg.

1 **(a)** Weigh an empty school bag.
(b) Estimate how much the
bag will weigh when it
contains

- a reading book, a maths book
  and a pencil case
- 3 library books, 4 exercise books
  and a pair of trainers.

(c) Use a spring balance or scales to check each estimate.

2 Put some objects into a school bag so that its total weight
is between 4 kg 800 g and 5 kg 100 g.

3 Write the weight of each object in grams.

(a) 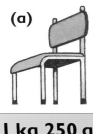   **(b)** 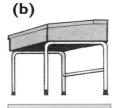   **(c)**    **(d)**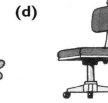

1 kg 250 g	**3 kg 125 g**	**4 kg 568 g**	**2 kg 379 g**

4 Write the weight of each object in kilograms and grams.

(a)    **(b)** 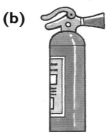   **(c)** 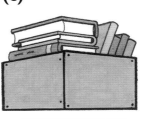   **(d)**

5482 g	**7634 g**	**9513 g**	**6747g**

5 Write each weight in another way.

(a) 7 kg 132 g **(b)** 8716 g **(c)** 4 kg 303 g **(d)** 6948 g
(e) 1 kg 255 g **(f)** 5681 g **(g)** 2 kg 569 g **(h)** 9074 g

1 Write each amount in millilitres.

(a)

(b)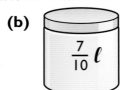

(e)

(f)

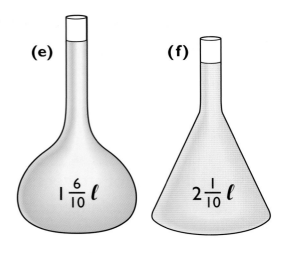

(c)

(d)

2 Write in order.

(a) Start with the smallest volume.

(b) Start with the largest volume.

3 How many millilitres of cream altogether are on each tray?

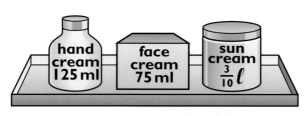 

4 Which **two** containers together hold

(a) $\frac{1}{2}$ litre   (b) 1 litre

(c) $1\frac{1}{2}$ litre   (d) $\frac{1}{4}$ litre?

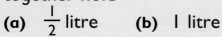 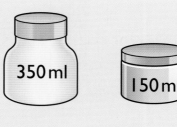 

5 Which **three** containers together hold

(a) 1 litre   (b) 2 litres?

You need containers like these,
a 1 litre measuring jar and a funnel.

1 **(a)** Estimate the capacity of each container and check by measuring.

Record your results in a table like this.

Container	Estimate	Measurement
A	about	about
B		
C		

(b) List the containers in order, starting with the greatest capacity.

2 Find the weight of
(a) 1 litre of water   **(b)** $\frac{1}{2}$ litre of water.

spoon   bucket   teapot   perfume bottle

can   bath   bowl   basin

1 List the items whose capacities Sally should measure in
   (a) millilitres   **(b)** litres.

2 Write two other items whose capacities should be measured in
   (a) millilitres   **(b)** litres.

3

100 ml   200 ml   350 ml   120 ml

What should be the reading on the scale if Sally **added** the contents of the

   (a) red bowl   **(b)** blue bowl
   (c) green bowl   **(d)** yellow bowl
   (e) red **and** green bowls
   (f) yellow **and** green bowls?

400 ml

300 ml

200 ml

4 How much liquid should Sally pour from the jug into the tub so that both have the same amount?

1ℓ 120 ml   960 ml

5

lemonade

1ℓ 200 ml

Sally empties the lemonade into a jug and a glass.
She pours 3 times as much into the jug as into the glass.

What volume of lemonade is in the **(a)** jug   **(b)** glass?

Use 'longs' like this.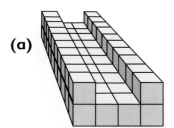

1 What is the volume in cm^3 of each long?

2 For each shape find
  • the number of longs used   • the volume in cm^3.

(a) **(b)**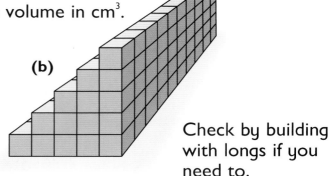

Check by building
with longs if you
need to.

3 • Build a **layer** of longs like this.

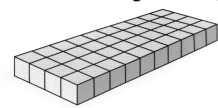

(a) What is its volume?

• How many layers are
needed to build a cuboid
with a volume of
(b) 120 cm^3 **(c)** 200 cm^3
(d) 1000 cm^3?

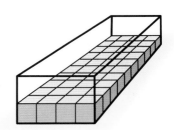

Work as a group.
Use 'flats' like this.

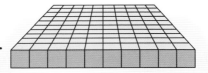

4 (a) What is the volume in cm^3 of each flat?
  (b) Build a cube using flats. How many flats did you use?
  (c) What is the volume of the cube in cm^3?

5 Use a hollow cube which has the **same** volume
as the cube you built with flats.

  (a) Fill the hollow cube with sand or water.
  (b) What is the volume of the sand/water
       in **millilitres**?
  (c) What is true about volumes of 1 cm^3 and 1 ml? Explain.

One **mile** is about
1600 metres.

1 About how many **kilometres**
is the distance to

(a) Melchester (b) Dirleton
(c) Penby?

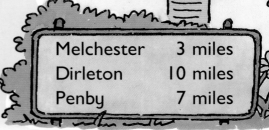

Melchester	3 miles
Dirleton	10 miles
Penby	7 miles

2

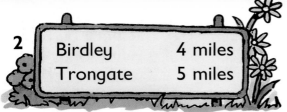

Birdley	4 miles
Trongate	5 miles

Chumley	6 kilometres
Winton	9 kilometres

Which town is further away?

(a) Birdley or Chumley (b) Trongate or Winton?

One **pint** is about
570 millilitres.

3 About how many millilitres are there in

(a) 2 pints (b) 5 pints?

4 Which is the greater volume,
3 pints of milk or
1 litres of milk?

5

One **gallon** is a little
less than 5 litres.

Which vehicle's fuel
tank has the smaller
capacity?

tank holds 8 gallons

tank holds 42 litres

 Preheat oven to
375°F (190°C)

Bake mixture for
a quarter of an hour

 Eat within 14 days of baking.

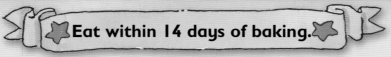

1 Write, in kilograms, the total weight of **fruit** used in the cake mixture.

2 Find the difference between the weights of flour and fruit used.

3 What is the **total** volume of **liquid** used?

4 What quantity of water is there in 12 tablespoons?

5 How many tablespoons of water are needed to make 170 ml?

6 The oven takes about 20 minutes to reach a temperature of 190°C. For about how many minutes has it been switched on when the baking is **complete**?

7 The cake mixture is placed in the oven at 11.55am. At what time should it be removed?

8 Should a cake baked on 28th March be eaten on 12th April? Explain.

Measure: mixed units, Problem solving and enquiry

Measure each length and breadth to the nearest centimetre.

1 Find the areas in cm^2.

(a)

(c)

(d)

(b)

2 Find the **approximate** areas in cm^2.

(a)

(b)

(c)

1 Find the approximate area of each papyrus piece in square centimetres.

(a)

(b)

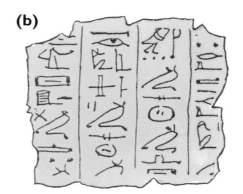

(c)

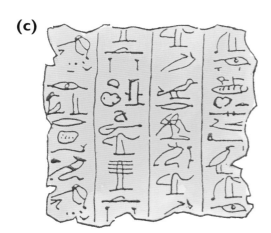

(d)

(e)

2 Draw 2 **different** papyrus pieces each with an area of about 24 cm².

3 The museum receives a new piece of papyrus.
Its area is about 100 cm².
The length of the piece is about 4 times the breadth.
What is its approximate length and breadth?

1   This is a plan of the Rexcon factory.
    Calculate the area of the

    (a)   Assembly Line
    (b)   Paint Shed
    (c)   Parts Store
    (d)   Whole factory.

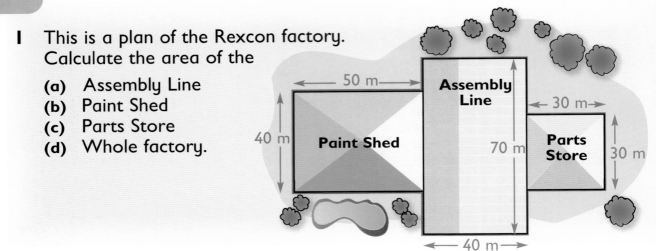

2   This is a plan of Mason's farm.
    Calculate the **total** area of the farm buildings.

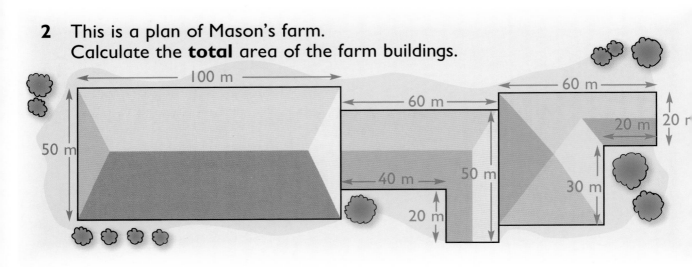

3   For each shape, **measure** side lengths then **calculate** the area.

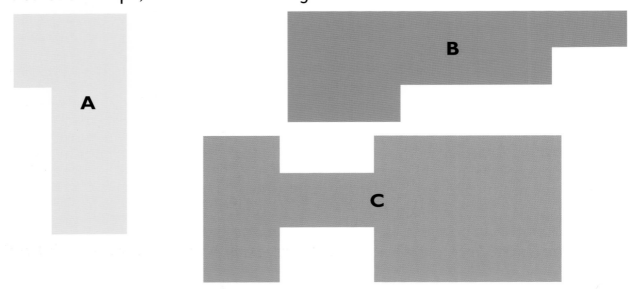

1 Find the area of each triangle in square centimetres.

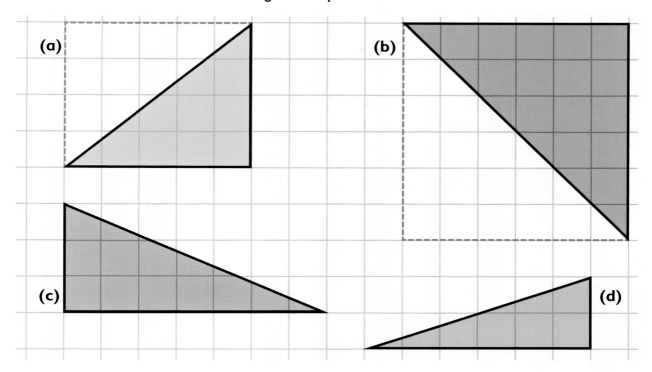

(a)

(b)

(c)

(d)

2 Find the area of each triangle in cm^2.

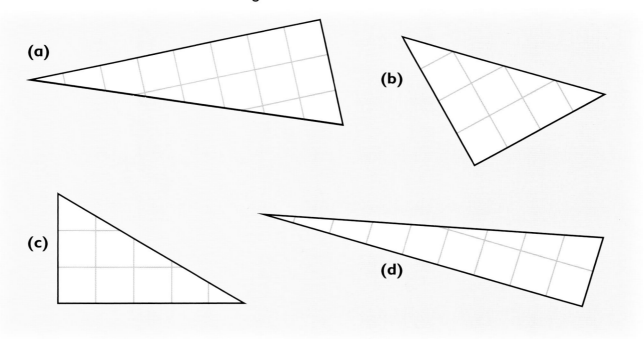

(a)

(b)

(c)

(d)

3 Draw two different right-angled triangles, each with an area of 20 cm^2.

1 Gordon is building a rectangular patio
4 metres long and 2 metres wide.
He is using square slabs with **50 centimetre** edges.
How many slabs does he need?

2 Gordon has to stain a wooden fence 18 m long and 2 m tall.
How many tins of *Woodstain* will he need to buy?
Explain.

3 A square plant label has a perimeter of 24 cm.
What is its area?

4 A rectangular vegetable patch has
a perimeter of 30 m.
Its **shorter** sides are each 5 m long.
What is the area of the vegetable patch?

5 Gordon has 48 square metres of turf to make
a rectangular lawn.
List the dimensions of different rectangles he
could make.

6 Gordon's plan shows a new flower bed.

- It is an **L**-shaped hexagon.
- Four of its sides are 2 m long and
  two of its sides are 4 m long.

Sketch Gordon's flower bed on squared paper
and find its area.

TOPIC ASSESSMENT

98

1 **(a)** Copy each design on squared paper.
(b) Complete each design so that it has two lines of symmetry.

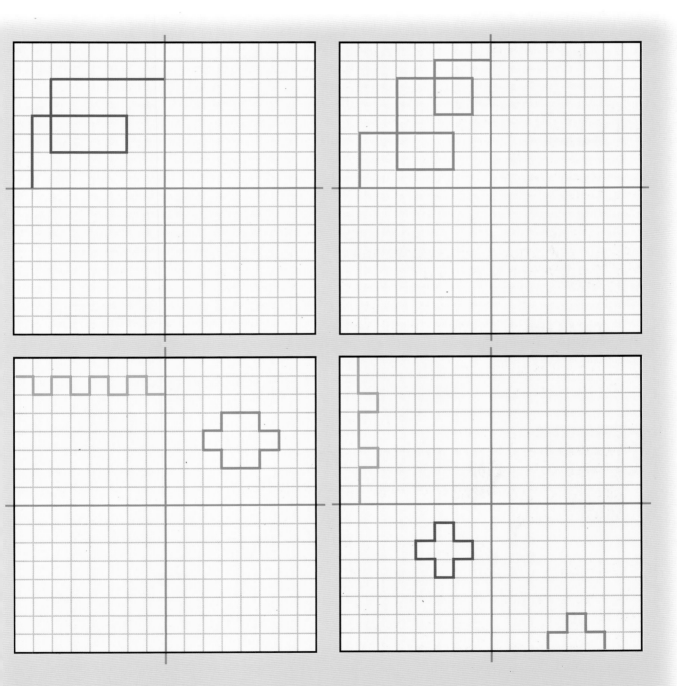

2 Draw and colour symetrical designs of your own.

1 Which triangles could each child be describing?

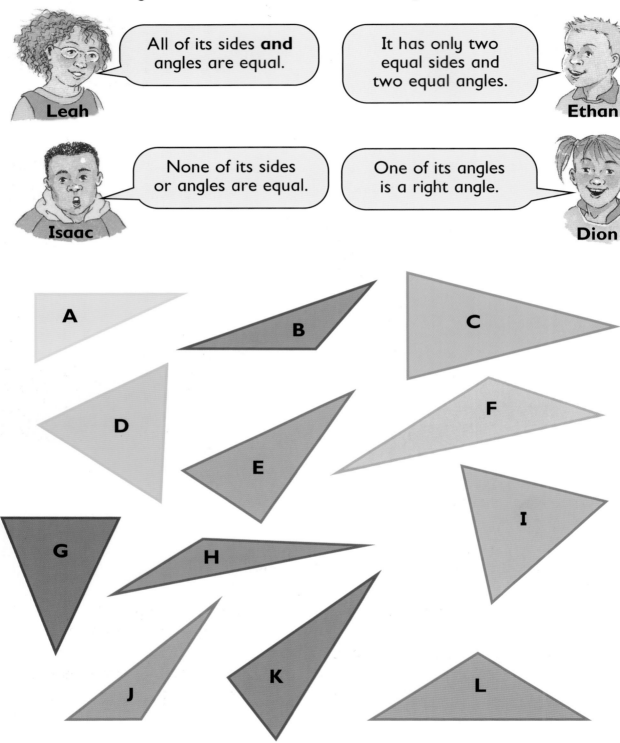

Leah: All of its sides **and** angles are equal.

Ethan: It has only two equal sides and two equal angles.

Isaac: None of its sides or angles are equal.

Dion: One of its angles is a right angle.

2 Draw another triangle which matches each description.

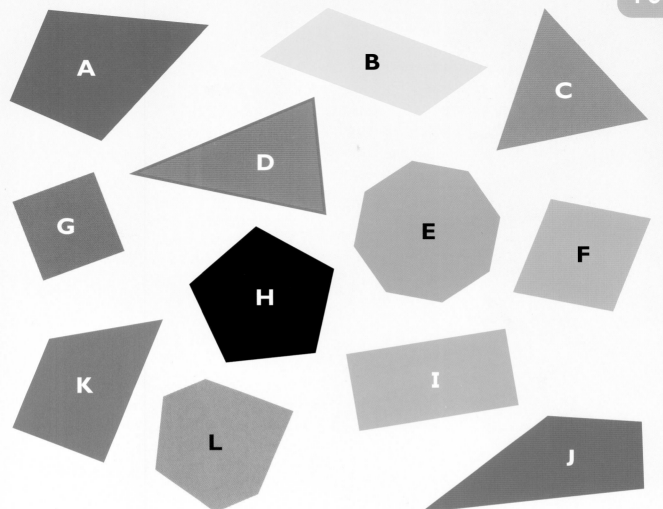

1 Which of the shapes

   (a)   are quadrilaterals

   (b)   have **all** sides equal

   (c)   have **only one** pair of **opposite** sides parallel

   (d)   has only one pair of opposite sides **equal**

   (e)   have only **two pairs** of opposite sides equal **and** parallel

   (f)   has more than two pairs of opposite sides equal and parallel

   (g)   have only one pair of **adjacent** sides equal

   (h)   are **not regular** and have only two pairs of adjacent sides equal

   (i)   has one pair of opposite sides parallel but **not** equal

   (j)   are parallelograms?

2   Name each shape.

1 Which of the shapes

    (a) have no lines of symmetry
    (b) have only one line of symmetry
    (c) have only two lines of symmetry
    (d) have more than two lines of symmetry?

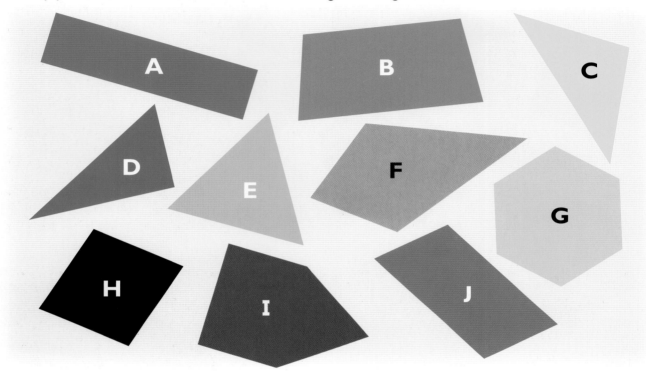

2 Which of the shapes

    (a) have **all** angles equal   **(b)** has **only** right angles
    (c) has only obtuse angles   **(d)** has only acute angles
    (e) has only two right angles   **(f)** has only one pair of equal angles
    (g) has right, acute **and** obtuse angles
    (h) has only one pair of **opposite** angles equal
    (i) have no right angles and only two pairs of opposite angles equal
    (j) has no right angles and only one pair of **adjacent** angles equal
    (k) has **no** equal angles?

3 Name each of the shapes.

4 Use squared paper. Draw a shape which has

    • two right angles
    • four obtuse angles
    • only one line of symmetry.

Use dotty paper.

1 Copy and continue each tiling.

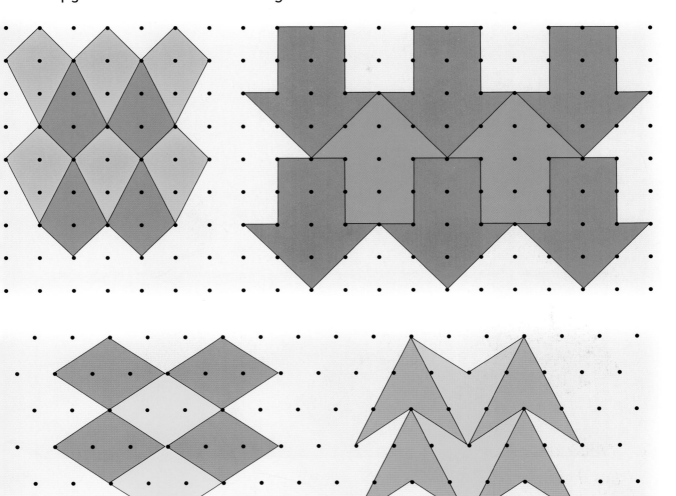

2 Make tilings using each of these shapes.

(a)   **(b)**

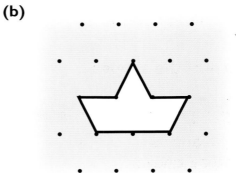

1 Use compasses and a ruler.
Make these circle patterns.

(a)

(b)

(c)

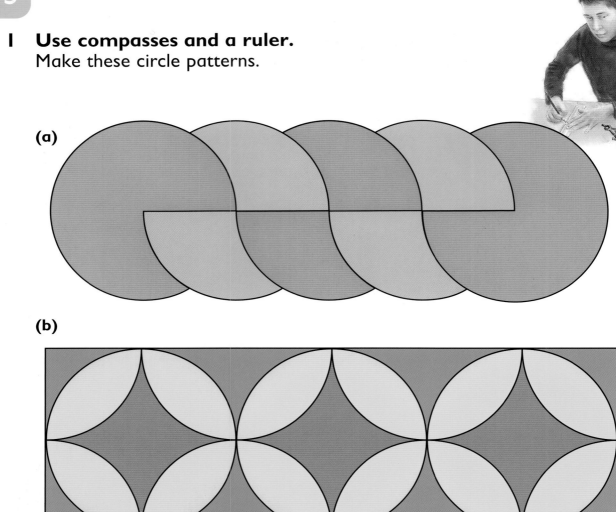
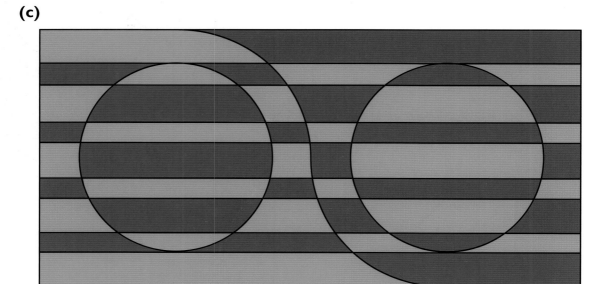

1 Start with **6 equally-spaced points on the circumference of a circle** each time. Make each of these designs.

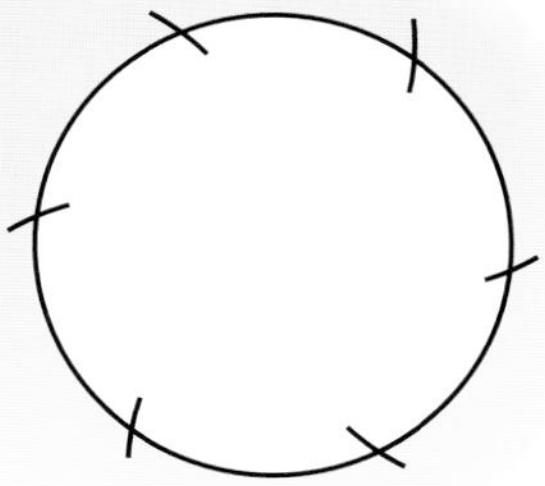

(a)

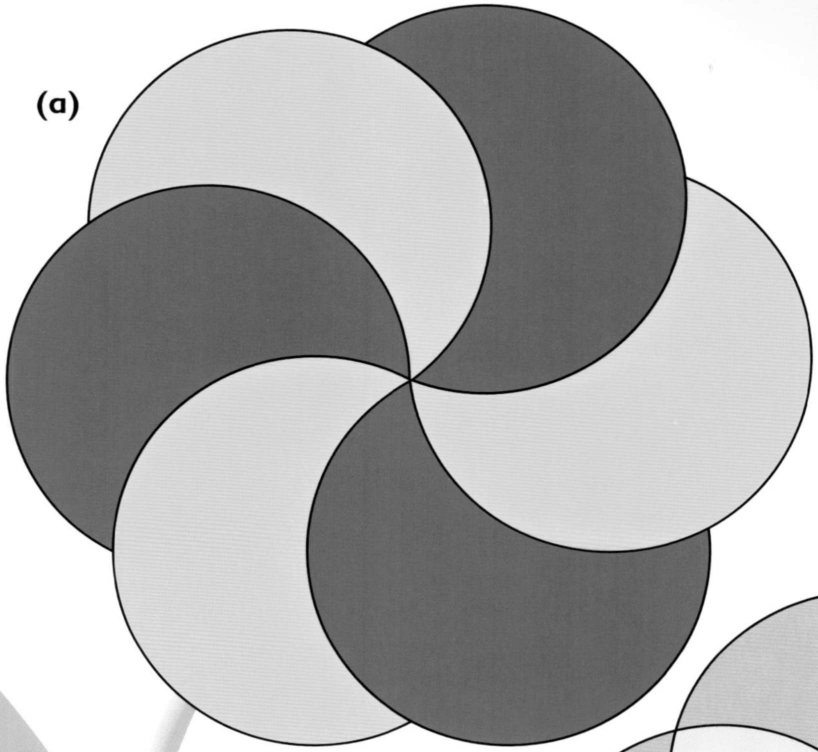

(b)

2 Investigate other designs you can make starting with 6 equally-spaced points on the circumference of a circle.

1   Use linking squares. Find which of these are nets of a cube.

(a)   **(b)**   **(c)**

(d)   **(e)**

(f)   **(g)**   **(h)**

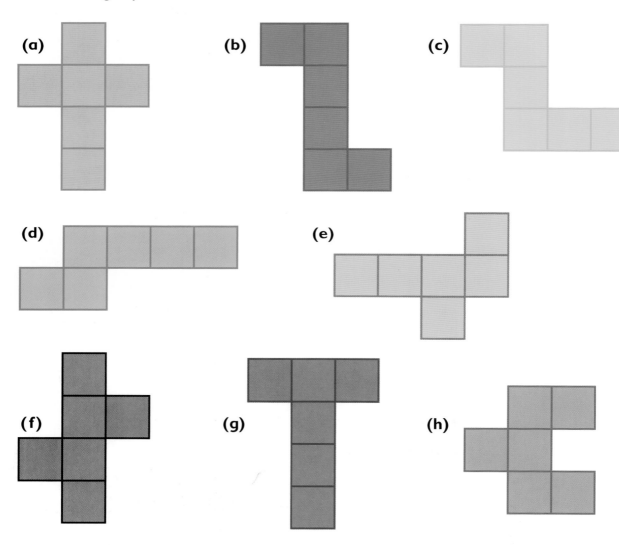

2   Join linking squares to make other nets of a cube.
    Draw these other nets on squared paper.

1 **(a)** For each net, name the 3D shape.

(b) Make each net then construct the shape to check.

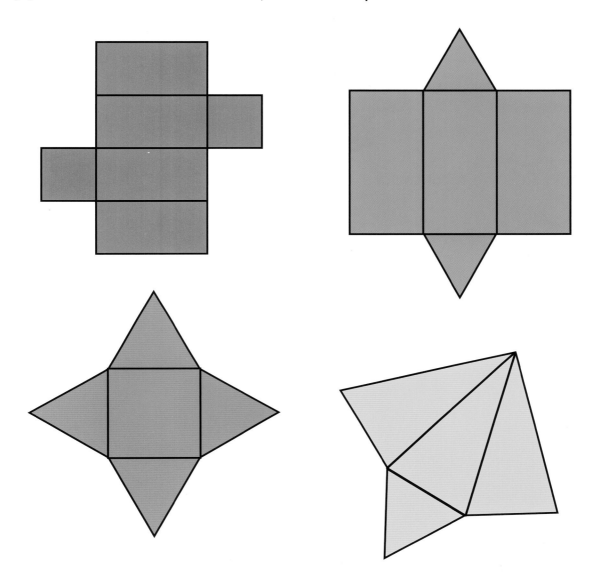

2 **(a)** Which nets do you **think** will make a box with no lid?

(b) Check by joining squares.

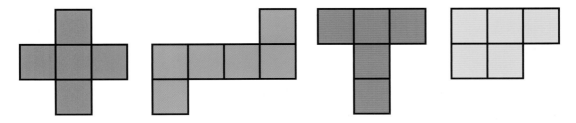

1 Calculate the total surface area of each shape.

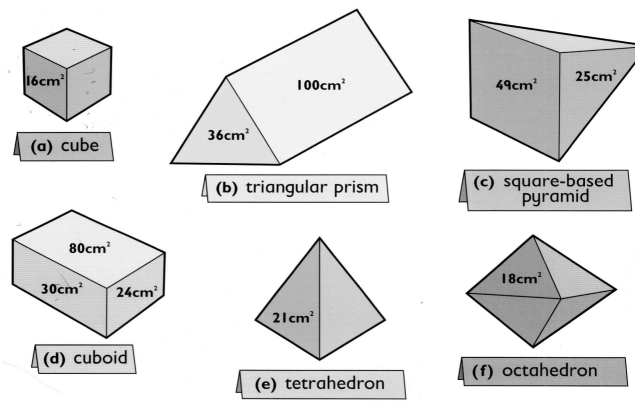

16cm²

(a) cube

100cm²

36cm²

(b) triangular prism

49cm²   25cm²

(c) square-based pyramid

80cm²

30cm²   24cm²

(d) cuboid

21cm²

(e) tetrahedron

18cm²

(f) octahedron

2 A 3D shape has
  • 2 square faces, each with sides 3 cm long
  • 4 rectangular faces, each with sides 5 cm long and 3 cm broad.

  (a) Name the 3D shape.
  (b) What is the **total surface area** of the shape in cm²?

3 The total surface area of a cube is 54 cm².
  What is the length of each of its edges?

In each question, check your answers, if you
need to, by building shapes using linking cubes.

1 How many cubes **do you think** are needed
to build each of these shapes?

(a)

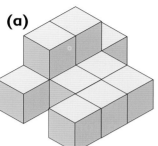

(b)

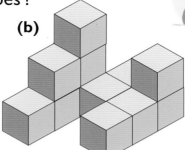

(c)

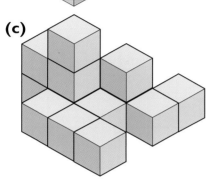

(d)

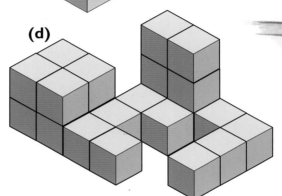

2 What is the least number of cubes needed to make each of these
shapes into a cuboid?

(a)

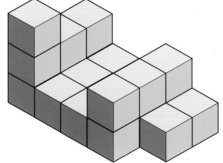

(b)

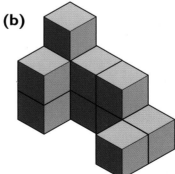

3 In each shape, what is the least number of cubes needed
to **cover and join** the coloured faces?

(a)

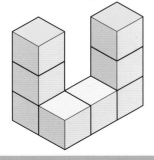

(b)

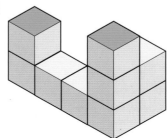

The chart shows the layout of the rocket **launch** complex.

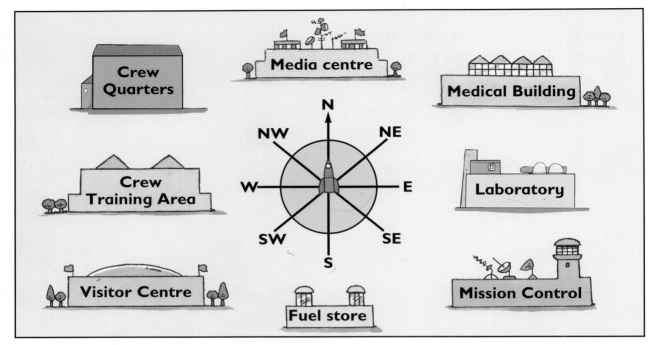

You are at the launch site at the centre of the complex.

1 Face the Laboratory.

What are you facing after you turn through

(a) 45° anti-clockwise   (b) 135° clockwise
(c) 225° clockwise   (d) 270° anti-clockwise?

2 Describe each turn in **two different ways**.

(a) Face the Visitor Centre. Turn to face the Crew Training Area.
(b) Face Mission Control. Turn to face the Media Centre.
(c) Face the Medical Building. Turn to face Mission Control.

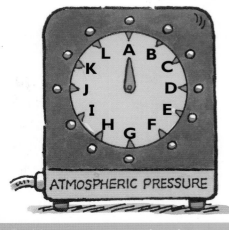

3 Through how many degrees **clockwise** does the pointer turn when it moves from

(a) facing A to face C
(b) facing C to face J
(c) facing E to face I
(d) facing K to face L
(e) facing J to face G?

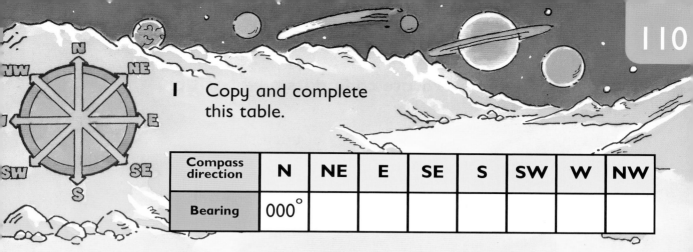

1 Copy and complete this table.

Compass direction	N	NE	E	SE	S	SW	W	NW
Bearing	000°							

2 The chart shows the layout of the rocket **landing** area.

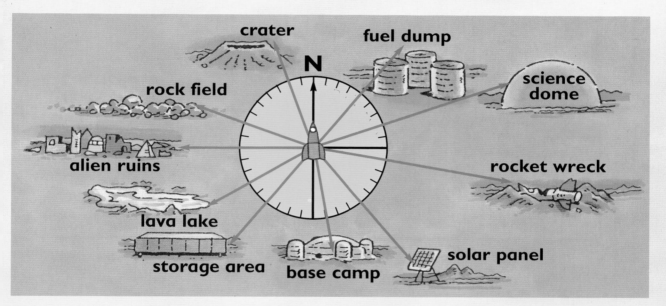

What is the bearing, from the landing site at the centre, of each place shown?

3 Each direction indicator is marked in 5° intervals.

Write the bearing, from the red dot, of each space buggy.

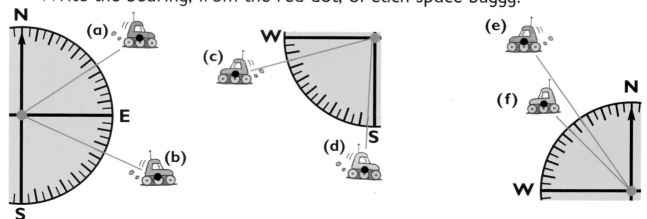

Trace each shape and rotate to find its new position.

I List the co-ordinates of the vertices of each shape
- in the position shown
- after it has rotated about the vertex marked with a dot.

(a) 90° clockwise

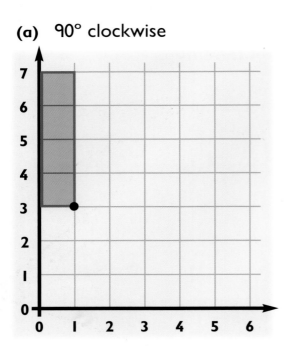

(b) 90° anti-clockwise

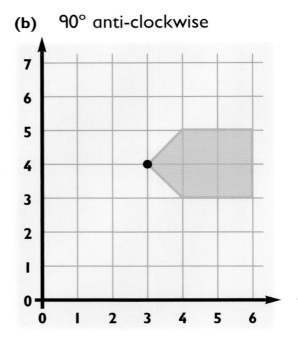

(c) 180° anti-clockwise

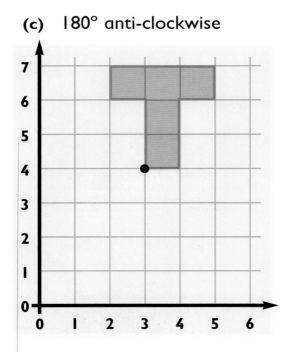

(d) 180° clockwise

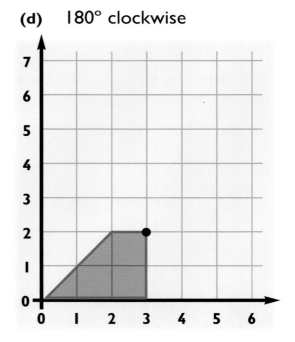

1 **(a)** **Estimate** the size of each angle **to the nearest 5°.**

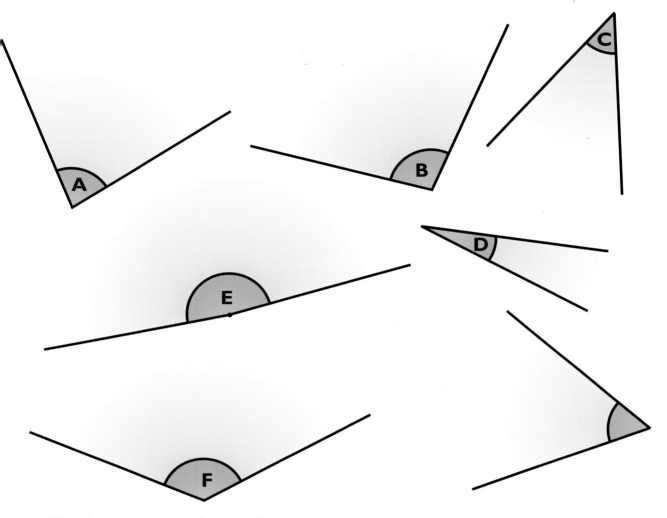

(b) Check by **measuring** with a protractor.

2 **Calculate** the size of each **blue** angle.

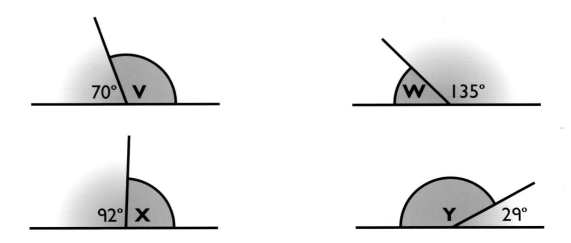

70° **V**

W 135°

92° **X**

Y 29°

The **trend graph** shows the number of swimmers at Parkvale Pool at 9 am each day for two weeks.

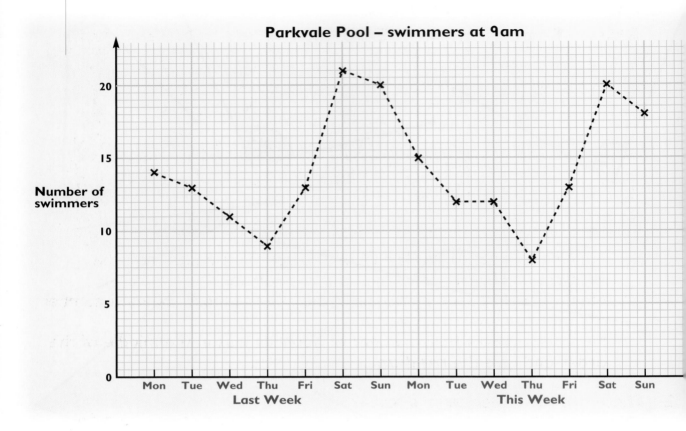

Parkvale Pool – swimmers at 9am

1 On which day and in which week was the number of swimmers

    (a) greatest   **(b)** smallest   **(c)** eleven   **(d)** eighteen?

2 How many swimmers were there on

    (a) Thursday last week   **(b)** Friday this week?

3 Write about the **trend** shown by the graph.

4 This table shows the number of swimmers who bought a ticket during each one hour session on Monday this week.

Time of session	09.00 -10.00	10.00 -11.00	11.00 -12.00	12.00 -13.00	13.00 -14.00	14.00 -15.00	15.00 -16.00	16.00 -17.00
Number of swimmers	15	18	16	38	35	21	9	23

    (a) Draw a trend graph using the data.
    (b) Write about the trend shown by the graph.

1 The children in the Class 6 Red team find out how many times they can bounce a basketball in one minute.

Alan	Bindu	Dave	Sammy	Dion	Anne	Luke
48	51	51	55	56	57	60

(a) Name the children who bounced the ball the smallest and the greatest number of times and give the **range.**

(b) Name the children who bounced the ball the most common number of times and give the **mode.**

(c) Name the child whose number of bounces was in the middle of the order and give the **median.**

2 These are the Green team's results.

54	62	55	58	60	50	60

(a) Write the numbers of bounces in order.

(b) Find   ● the range   ● the mode   ● the median.

3 These are the results for the 11 children in the Blue team.

60	54	52	49	52	60
	57	58	50	60	64

(a) Write the numbers of bounces in order.

(b) Find   ● the range   ● the mode   ● the median.

4 (a) Write all 25 results for the red, green and blue teams in order.

(b) Find   ● the range   ● the mode   ● the median.

The Class 6 Red team measure the
height they can make a ball bounce.
The results are shown in the **bar chart.**

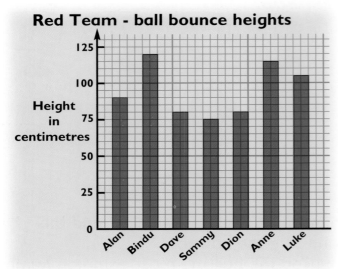

1 Who made the ball bounce **(a)** highest **(b)** lowest?

2 For the Red team's results give
(a) the range **(b)** the mode **(c)** the median.

3 Each time the ball is thrown into the
basket 3 points are scored.
The points scored in one minute by
the Green team were:

30   21   15   30   27   30   15

For the Green team's results, find
(a) the range **(b)** the mode **(c)** the median.

4 For each of these teams' results, find
(a) the range **(b)** the mode **(c)** the median.

<table>
<tr><td>**Red team**
18 18 21 27
24 18 21</td><td>**Yellow team**
21 30 24 24 15
18 15 18 24</td><td>**Orange team**
12 21 24 18 9
21 12 9 18
12 6 21 12</td></tr>
</table>

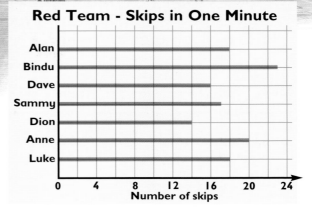

Red Team - Skips in One Minute

The **bar line chart** shows how many times the Class 6 Red team skipped in one minute.

I   (a) How many skips were made by • Anne   • Sammy?
    (b) Find the total number of skips for the whole team.
    (c) Find the **mean** number of skips by dividing the total number of skips by the number of children in the team.
    (d) Name the children whose number of skips was
         • less than the mean • greater than the mean • equal to the mean.

2   (a) Find the total number of skips for the Green team.
    (b) Calculate the mean number of skips per child.
    (c) Name the children whose number of skips was
         • above the mean • below the mean.

Green Team - Skips in One Minute

Steve - 22   Lisa - 20   Paul - 18
Nazir - 15   Dianne - 21
Joan - 17   Sheena - 20

3

These are the numbers of skips for the Blue team.

18 17 24 23
19 18 24
17 22 20 18

    (a) What is • the range • the mode • the median?
    (b) Find the mean number of skips per child.
    (c) For **how many** children was the number of skips
         • above the mean • below the mean • equal to the mean?

1 This **compound bar chart** shows the values of the book tokens given to five girls on their birthdays.

Birthday Book Tokens

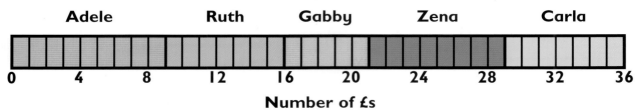

(a) What is the total value of the girls' book tokens?

(b) What is the value of the book token given to
- Adele • Carla • Gabby • Zena • Ruth?

(c) What fraction of the total value is the value of Adele's token?

(d) Use $\frac{1}{2}$-centimetre squared paper. Draw a **bar line chart** to show the same information as the compound bar chart.

2 These two graphs show the same information about the values of the gift vouchers given to five boys on their birthdays.

Birthday Gift Vouchers

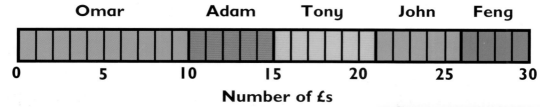

(a) What is the total value of the vouchers?

(b) Whose voucher is $\frac{1}{3}$ of the total value?

(c) Which children's vouchers are of equal value?

(d) What is the value of each boy's voucher?

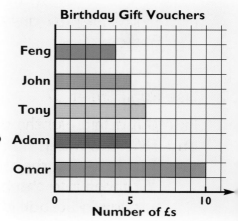

3 For each part of question **2**, which graph shows the answer more clearly?

Is it true that five eighths of the children in Year 6 are between 139 centimetres and 160 centimetres tall?

Some children carry out a survey to find the answer to their Headteacher's challenge question.

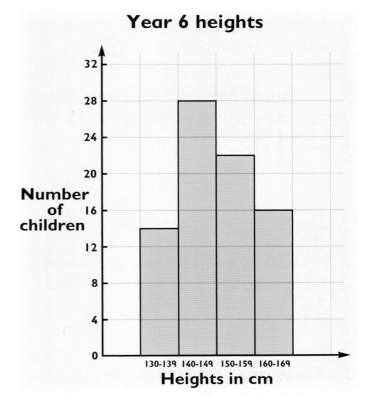

Year 6 heights

Number of children

Heights in cm

130-139 140-149 150-159 160-169

1 **(a)** How many class intervals are there in the graph?

(b) Which class interval contains
  • the greatest number of children • the smallest number of children?

(c) In which class interval is
  • the shortest height • the tallest height?

(d) How many children are
  • shorter than 140 cm • between 149 cm and 160 cm tall?

(e) What fraction of the children are
  • taller than 159 cm • between 139 cm and 150 cm tall?

(f) What is **your** answer to the Headteacher's challenge question? Explain.

2 Use Pupil Sheet 57.

Find out if five eighths of the children in **your** class are between 139 cm and 160 cm tall by
  • measuring their heights to the nearest centimetre
  • completing the frequency table
  • drawing a bar chart of the data.

Baxdale School's Shoebox Project helps to provide classroom items for schools in developing countries.

The children in Class 6 calculate the amount of money each group needs to collect to fill a shoebox with classroom items.

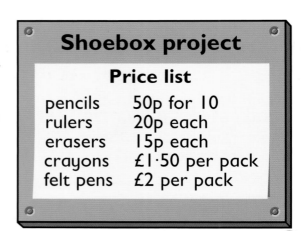

Shoebox project

Price list

pencils	50p for 10
rulers	20p each
erasers	15p each
crayons	£1·50 per pack
felt pens	£2 per pack

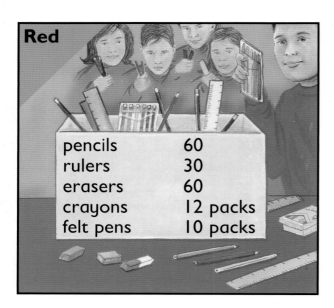

Red

pencils	60
rulers	30
erasers	60
crayons	12 packs
felt pens	10 packs

Yellow

pencils	90
rulers	60
erasers	30
crayons	10 packs
felt pens	12 packs

Blue

pencils	120
rulers	45
erasers	45
crayons	6 packs
felt pens	5 packs

Green

pencils	100
rulers	60
erasers	60
crayons	5 packs
felt pens	6 packs

Use the Spreadsheets on Pupil Sheet 58.

I **(a)** Complete a table like this for each of the four groups.

group	pencils	rulers	erasers	crayons	felt pens	
Number						
Cost each						**Total**
Total cost						

(b) Which group needs to collect ● most money ● least money?

(c) There are 5 children in each group. Find the mean amount of money that needs to be collected per child in each group.

2 The Red and Blue groups decide to change the contents of their shoeboxes.

The Red group wants
- 20 more pencils
- 20 fewer erasers.

The Blue group wants
- 40 fewer pencils
- 5 more packs of felt pens.

(a) Alter your tables to include this information.
(b) Find the mean amount of money that needs to be collected per child in ● the Red group ● the Blue group.

3 The Yellow and Green groups each add an extra item to their shoebox.

The Yellow group adds 8 tubes of paint at £1·75 each.
The Green group adds 12 glue sticks at £1·25 each.

Alter your tables to include this information.

	Svensun 5	Morten	Rodex	Sherwood
Talk time	300 min	130 min	180 min	300 min
Number of ring tones	21	43	20	24
Internet access	✓	no access	no access	✓ ✓
Accessories	✓	✓ ✓	✓	✓ ✓

	Quad	Venta	Norlund	Svensun 12
Talk time	210 min	210 min	240 min	480 min
Number of ring tones	14	48	35	20
Internet access	✓	✓	✓	✓
Accessories	✓	✓ ✓	✓ ✓ ✓	✓

Key :

Internet access				Accessories		
built in	with cable	with modem		hands free	new covers	fun pack

1 Name the mobile telephone models which

   (a) have exactly 210 minutes of talk time
   (b) have between 225 minutes and 325 minutes of talk time
   (c) have more than 40 different ring tones
   (d) have no access to the Internet
   (e) can access the Internet with a modem
   (f) can have new covers attached.

2 Which accessory is available with every one of the phones?

3 Which phone model has all the features listed?

(a) M.P.S.
   - exactly 20 ring tones
   - a hands-free kit
   - Internet access

(b) M.P.S.
   - more than 30 ring tones
   - Internet access
   - new covers

(c) M.P.S.
   - access to the Internet with a cable attached
   - exactly 300 minutes of talk time
   - more than 22 ring tones

4 Ask your teacher if you can enter the information into a computer database.

The children in your class will be helping in the café.

**Baxdale School Fayre
Saturday 2nd April
Opens 9.30am**

What chance does each event have of happening at Baxdale School Fayre?

Write | no chance | **or** | poor chance | **or** | even chance | **or** | good chance | **or** | certain |.

A You will go to the Fayre by helicopter.

B You will see a classmate.

C Something will be spilled.

D All of the scones will be sold.

E No biscuits will be sold.

F It will rain.